The Groom Checklists
GroomHandBooks3

ISBN-13: 978-1977930941

ISBN-10: 1977930948

Groomsmen and Ushers' Checklist

PRE-WEDDING PLANNING PROCESS

- Participate in party for the groom, if there is one
- Pay for own wedding attire and transportation to the wedding
- Contribute to the ushers' gift to the groom. Usually gives an individual gift to the couple expected to attend the rehearsal and the rehearsal dinner

WEDDING DAY

- Review any special seating situations with the head usher before the ceremony begins
- Greets guests as they arrive
- Seat the eldest women first if a group of guests arrive simultaneously
- Ask guests whether they are to be seated on the bride's side or the groom's side
- Offer their right arm to female guests (with the guest's escort walking behind) or ask couples to follow behind (leading couple to their seat)
- Walk to the left side of a male guest
- Hand each guest a program when they are seated
- Put the aisle runner in place after guests are seated and before the processional begins
- Know the order of seating per tradition such as special guests, grandmothers of the bride and groom, and bride's mother last
- Remove pew ribbons, one row at a time, after the ceremony
- Close windows and check pews for programs or articles left behind after the ceremony
- Are prepared to direct guests to the reception site (having extra maps available, if used)
- Look after elderly relatives or friends
- Participate in garter ceremony, if there is one, and encourage other single men to participate

POST WEDDING

- Coordinate return of rented apparel with head usher or best man

Notes:

Groomsmen and Ushers' Checklist

PRE-WEDDING PLANNING PROCESS

- Participate in party for the groom, if there is one
- Pay for own wedding attire and transportation to the wedding
- Contribute to the ushers' gift to the groom. Usually gives an individual gift to the couple expected to attend the rehearsal and the rehearsal dinner

WEDDING DAY

- Review any special seating situations with the head usher before the ceremony begins
- Greets guests as they arrive
- Seat the eldest women first if a group of guests arrive simultaneously
- Ask guests whether they are to be seated on the bride's side or the groom's side
- Offer their right arm to female guests (with the guest's escort walking behind) or ask couples to follow behind (leading couple to their seat)
- Walk to the left side of a male guest
- Hand each guest a program when they are seated
- Put the aisle runner in place after guests are seated and before the processional begins
- Know the order of seating per tradition such as special guests, grandmothers of the bride and groom, and bride's mother last
- Remove pew ribbons, one row at a time, after the ceremony
- Close windows and check pews for programs or articles left behind after the ceremony
- Are prepared to direct guests to the reception site (having extra maps available, if used)
- Look after elderly relatives or friends
- Participate in garter ceremony, if there is one, and encourage other single men to participate

POST WEDDING

- Coordinate return of rented apparel with head usher or best man

Notes:

Groomsmen and Ushers' Checklist

PRE-WEDDING PLANNING PROCESS

- Participate in party for the groom, if there is one
- Pay for own wedding attire and transportation to the wedding
- Contribute to the ushers' gift to the groom. Usually gives an individual gift to the couple expected to attend the rehearsal and the rehearsal dinner

WEDDING DAY

- Review any special seating situations with the head usher before the ceremony begins
- Greets guests as they arrive
- Seat the eldest women first if a group of guests arrive simultaneously
- Ask guests whether they are to be seated on the bride's side or the groom's side
- Offer their right arm to female guests (with the guest's escort walking behind) or ask couples to follow behind (leading couple to their seat)
- Walk to the left side of a male guest
- Hand each guest a program when they are seated
- Put the aisle runner in place after guests are seated and before the processional begins
- Know the order of seating per tradition such as special guests, grandmothers of the bride and groom, and bride's mother last
- Remove pew ribbons, one row at a time, after the ceremony
- Close windows and check pews for programs or articles left behind after the ceremony
- Are prepared to direct guests to the reception site (having extra maps available, if used)
- Look after elderly relatives or friends
- Participate in garter ceremony, if there is one, and encourage other single men to participate

POST WEDDING

- Coordinate return of rented apparel with head usher or best man

Notes:

Groomsmen and Ushers' Checklist

PRE-WEDDING PLANNING PROCESS

- Participate in party for the groom, if there is one
- Pay for own wedding attire and transportation to the wedding
- Contribute to the ushers' gift to the groom. Usually gives an individual gift to the couple expected to attend the rehearsal and the rehearsal dinner

WEDDING DAY

- Review any special seating situations with the head usher before the ceremony begins
- Greets guests as they arrive
- Seat the eldest women first if a group of guests arrive simultaneously
- Ask guests whether they are to be seated on the bride's side or the groom's side
- Offer their right arm to female guests (with the guest's escort walking behind) or ask couples to follow behind (leading couple to their seat)
- Walk to the left side of a male guest
- Hand each guest a program when they are seated
- Put the aisle runner in place after guests are seated and before the processional begins
- Know the order of seating per tradition such as special guests, grandmothers of the bride and groom, and bride's mother last
- Remove pew ribbons, one row at a time, after the ceremony
- Close windows and check pews for programs or articles left behind after the ceremony
- Are prepared to direct guests to the reception site (having extra maps available, if used)
- Look after elderly relatives or friends
- Participate in garter ceremony, if there is one, and encourage other single men to participate

POST WEDDING

- Coordinate return of rented apparel with head usher or best man

Notes:

Groomsmen and Ushers' Checklist

PRE-WEDDING PLANNING PROCESS

- Participate in party for the groom, if there is one
- Pay for own wedding attire and transportation to the wedding
- Contribute to the ushers' gift to the groom. Usually gives an individual gift to the couple expected to attend the rehearsal and the rehearsal dinner

WEDDING DAY

- Review any special seating situations with the head usher before the ceremony begins
- Greets guests as they arrive
- Seat the eldest women first if a group of guests arrive simultaneously
- Ask guests whether they are to be seated on the bride's side or the groom's side
- Offer their right arm to female guests (with the guest's escort walking behind) or ask couples to follow behind (leading couple to their seat)
- Walk to the left side of a male guest
- Hand each guest a program when they are seated
- Put the aisle runner in place after guests are seated and before the processional begins
- Know the order of seating per tradition such as special guests, grandmothers of the bride and groom, and bride's mother last
- Remove pew ribbons, one row at a time, after the ceremony
- Close windows and check pews for programs or articles left behind after the ceremony
- Are prepared to direct guests to the reception site (having extra maps available, if used)
- Look after elderly relatives or friends
- Participate in garter ceremony, if there is one, and encourage other single men to participate

POST WEDDING

- Coordinate return of rented apparel with head usher or best man

Notes:
____
____
____
____

Groomsmen and Ushers' Checklist

PRE-WEDDING PLANNING PROCESS

- Participate in party for the groom, if there is one
- Pay for own wedding attire and transportation to the wedding
- Contribute to the ushers' gift to the groom. Usually gives an individual gift to the couple expected to attend the rehearsal and the rehearsal dinner

WEDDING DAY

- Review any special seating situations with the head usher before the ceremony begins
- Greets guests as they arrive
- Seat the eldest women first if a group of guests arrive simultaneously
- Ask guests whether they are to be seated on the bride's side or the groom's side
- Offer their right arm to female guests (with the guest's escort walking behind) or ask couples to follow behind (leading couple to their seat)
- Walk to the left side of a male guest
- Hand each guest a program when they are seated
- Put the aisle runner in place after guests are seated and before the processional begins
- Know the order of seating per tradition such as special guests, grandmothers of the bride and groom, and bride's mother last
- Remove pew ribbons, one row at a time, after the ceremony
- Close windows and check pews for programs or articles left behind after the ceremony
- Are prepared to direct guests to the reception site (having extra maps available, if used)
- Look after elderly relatives or friends
- Participate in garter ceremony, if there is one, and encourage other single men to participate

POST WEDDING

- Coordinate return of rented apparel with head usher or best man

Notes:
____
____
____
____

Groomsmen and Ushers' Checklist

PRE-WEDDING PLANNING PROCESS

- Participate in party for the groom, if there is one
- Pay for own wedding attire and transportation to the wedding
- Contribute to the ushers' gift to the groom. Usually gives an individual gift to the couple expected to attend the rehearsal and the rehearsal dinner

WEDDING DAY

- Review any special seating situations with the head usher before the ceremony begins
- Greets guests as they arrive
- Seat the eldest women first if a group of guests arrive simultaneously
- Ask guests whether they are to be seated on the bride's side or the groom's side
- Offer their right arm to female guests (with the guest's escort walking behind) or ask couples to follow behind (leading couple to their seat)
- Walk to the left side of a male guest
- Hand each guest a program when they are seated
- Put the aisle runner in place after guests are seated and before the processional begins
- Know the order of seating per tradition such as special guests, grandmothers of the bride and groom, and bride's mother last
- Remove pew ribbons, one row at a time, after the ceremony
- Close windows and check pews for programs or articles left behind after the ceremony
- Are prepared to direct guests to the reception site (having extra maps available, if used)
- Look after elderly relatives or friends
- Participate in garter ceremony, if there is one, and encourage other single men to participate

POST WEDDING

- Coordinate return of rented apparel with head usher or best man

---

Notes:
____
____
____

Groomsmen and Ushers' Checklist

PRE-WEDDING PLANNING PROCESS

- Participate in party for the groom, if there is one
- Pay for own wedding attire and transportation to the wedding
- Contribute to the ushers' gift to the groom. Usually gives an individual gift to the couple expected to attend the rehearsal and the rehearsal dinner

WEDDING DAY

- Review any special seating situations with the head usher before the ceremony begins
- Greets guests as they arrive
- Seat the eldest women first if a group of guests arrive simultaneously
- Ask guests whether they are to be seated on the bride's side or the groom's side
- Offer their right arm to female guests (with the guest's escort walking behind) or ask couples to follow behind (leading couple to their seat)
- Walk to the left side of a male guest
- Hand each guest a program when they are seated
- Put the aisle runner in place after guests are seated and before the processional begins
- Know the order of seating per tradition such as special guests, grandmothers of the bride and groom, and bride's mother last
- Remove pew ribbons, one row at a time, after the ceremony
- Close windows and check pews for programs or articles left behind after the ceremony
- Are prepared to direct guests to the reception site (having extra maps available, if used)
- Look after elderly relatives or friends
- Participate in garter ceremony, if there is one, and encourage other single men to participate

POST WEDDING

- Coordinate return of rented apparel with head usher or best man

Notes:

Groomsmen and Ushers' Checklist

PRE-WEDDING PLANNING PROCESS

- Participate in party for the groom, if there is one
- Pay for own wedding attire and transportation to the wedding
- Contribute to the ushers' gift to the groom. Usually gives an individual gift to the couple expected to attend the rehearsal and the rehearsal dinner

WEDDING DAY

- Review any special seating situations with the head usher before the ceremony begins
- Greets guests as they arrive
- Seat the eldest women first if a group of guests arrive simultaneously
- Ask guests whether they are to be seated on the bride's side or the groom's side
- Offer their right arm to female guests (with the guest's escort walking behind) or ask couples to follow behind (leading couple to their seat)
- Walk to the left side of a male guest
- Hand each guest a program when they are seated
- Put the aisle runner in place after guests are seated and before the processional begins
- Know the order of seating per tradition such as special guests, grandmothers of the bride and groom, and bride's mother last
- Remove pew ribbons, one row at a time, after the ceremony
- Close windows and check pews for programs or articles left behind after the ceremony
- Are prepared to direct guests to the reception site (having extra maps available, if used)
- Look after elderly relatives or friends
- Participate in garter ceremony, if there is one, and encourage other single men to participate

POST WEDDING

- Coordinate return of rented apparel with head usher or best man

Notes:
____
____
____
____

Groomsmen and Ushers' Checklist

PRE-WEDDING PLANNING PROCESS

- Participate in party for the groom, if there is one
- Pay for own wedding attire and transportation to the wedding
- Contribute to the ushers' gift to the groom. Usually gives an individual gift to the couple expected to attend the rehearsal and the rehearsal dinner

WEDDING DAY

- Review any special seating situations with the head usher before the ceremony begins
- Greets guests as they arrive
- Seat the eldest women first if a group of guests arrive simultaneously
- Ask guests whether they are to be seated on the bride's side or the groom's side
- Offer their right arm to female guests (with the guest's escort walking behind) or ask couples to follow behind (leading couple to their seat)
- Walk to the left side of a male guest
- Hand each guest a program when they are seated
- Put the aisle runner in place after guests are seated and before the processional begins
- Know the order of seating per tradition such as special guests, grandmothers of the bride and groom, and bride's mother last
- Remove pew ribbons, one row at a time, after the ceremony
- Close windows and check pews for programs or articles left behind after the ceremony
- Are prepared to direct guests to the reception site (having extra maps available, if used)
- Look after elderly relatives or friends
- Participate in garter ceremony, if there is one, and encourage other single men to participate

POST WEDDING

- Coordinate return of rented apparel with head usher or best man

Notes:

Groomsmen and Ushers' Checklist

PRE-WEDDING PLANNING PROCESS

- Participate in party for the groom, if there is one
- Pay for own wedding attire and transportation to the wedding
- Contribute to the ushers' gift to the groom. Usually gives an individual gift to the couple expected to attend the rehearsal and the rehearsal dinner

WEDDING DAY

- Review any special seating situations with the head usher before the ceremony begins
- Greets guests as they arrive
- Seat the eldest women first if a group of guests arrive simultaneously
- Ask guests whether they are to be seated on the bride's side or the groom's side
- Offer their right arm to female guests (with the guest's escort walking behind) or ask couples to follow behind (leading couple to their seat)
- Walk to the left side of a male guest
- Hand each guest a program when they are seated
- Put the aisle runner in place after guests are seated and before the processional begins
- Know the order of seating per tradition such as special guests, grandmothers of the bride and groom, and bride's mother last
- Remove pew ribbons, one row at a time, after the ceremony
- Close windows and check pews for programs or articles left behind after the ceremony
- Are prepared to direct guests to the reception site (having extra maps available, if used)
- Look after elderly relatives or friends
- Participate in garter ceremony, if there is one, and encourage other single men to participate

POST WEDDING

- Coordinate return of rented apparel with head usher or best man

Notes:
____
____
____
____

Groomsmen and Ushers' Checklist

PRE-WEDDING PLANNING PROCESS

- Participate in party for the groom, if there is one
- Pay for own wedding attire and transportation to the wedding
- Contribute to the ushers' gift to the groom. Usually gives an individual gift to the couple expected to attend the rehearsal and the rehearsal dinner

WEDDING DAY

- Review any special seating situations with the head usher before the ceremony begins
- Greets guests as they arrive
- Seat the eldest women first if a group of guests arrive simultaneously
- Ask guests whether they are to be seated on the bride's side or the groom's side
- Offer their right arm to female guests (with the guest's escort walking behind) or ask couples to follow behind (leading couple to their seat)
- Walk to the left side of a male guest
- Hand each guest a program when they are seated
- Put the aisle runner in place after guests are seated and before the processional begins
- Know the order of seating per tradition such as special guests, grandmothers of the bride and groom, and bride's mother last
- Remove pew ribbons, one row at a time, after the ceremony
- Close windows and check pews for programs or articles left behind after the ceremony
- Are prepared to direct guests to the reception site (having extra maps available, if used)
- Look after elderly relatives or friends
- Participate in garter ceremony, if there is one, and encourage other single men to participate

POST WEDDING

- Coordinate return of rented apparel with head usher or best man

Notes:

Groomsmen and Ushers' Checklist

PRE-WEDDING PLANNING PROCESS

- Participate in party for the groom, if there is one
- Pay for own wedding attire and transportation to the wedding
- Contribute to the ushers' gift to the groom. Usually gives an individual gift to the couple expected to attend the rehearsal and the rehearsal dinner

WEDDING DAY

- Review any special seating situations with the head usher before the ceremony begins
- Greets guests as they arrive
- Seat the eldest women first if a group of guests arrive simultaneously
- Ask guests whether they are to be seated on the bride's side or the groom's side
- Offer their right arm to female guests (with the guest's escort walking behind) or ask couples to follow behind (leading couple to their seat)
- Walk to the left side of a male guest
- Hand each guest a program when they are seated
- Put the aisle runner in place after guests are seated and before the processional begins
- Know the order of seating per tradition such as special guests, grandmothers of the bride and groom, and bride's mother last
- Remove pew ribbons, one row at a time, after the ceremony
- Close windows and check pews for programs or articles left behind after the ceremony
- Are prepared to direct guests to the reception site (having extra maps available, if used)
- Look after elderly relatives or friends
- Participate in garter ceremony, if there is one, and encourage other single men to participate

POST WEDDING

- Coordinate return of rented apparel with head usher or best man

Notes:

Groomsmen and Ushers' Checklist

PRE-WEDDING PLANNING PROCESS

- Participate in party for the groom, if there is one
- Pay for own wedding attire and transportation to the wedding
- Contribute to the ushers' gift to the groom. Usually gives an individual gift to the couple expected to attend the rehearsal and the rehearsal dinner

WEDDING DAY

- Review any special seating situations with the head usher before the ceremony begins
- Greets guests as they arrive
- Seat the eldest women first if a group of guests arrive simultaneously
- Ask guests whether they are to be seated on the bride's side or the groom's side
- Offer their right arm to female guests (with the guest's escort walking behind) or ask couples to follow behind (leading couple to their seat)
- Walk to the left side of a male guest
- Hand each guest a program when they are seated
- Put the aisle runner in place after guests are seated and before the processional begins
- Know the order of seating per tradition such as special guests, grandmothers of the bride and groom, and bride's mother last
- Remove pew ribbons, one row at a time, after the ceremony
- Close windows and check pews for programs or articles left behind after the ceremony
- Are prepared to direct guests to the reception site (having extra maps available, if used)
- Look after elderly relatives or friends
- Participate in garter ceremony, if there is one, and encourage other single men to participate

POST WEDDING

- Coordinate return of rented apparel with head usher or best man

Notes: ____

____

____

____

Groomsmen and Ushers' Checklist

PRE-WEDDING PLANNING PROCESS

- Participate in party for the groom, if there is one
- Pay for own wedding attire and transportation to the wedding
- Contribute to the ushers' gift to the groom. Usually gives an individual gift to the couple expected to attend the rehearsal and the rehearsal dinner

WEDDING DAY

- Review any special seating situations with the head usher before the ceremony begins
- Greets guests as they arrive
- Seat the eldest women first if a group of guests arrive simultaneously
- Ask guests whether they are to be seated on the bride's side or the groom's side
- Offer their right arm to female guests (with the guest's escort walking behind) or ask couples to follow behind (leading couple to their seat)
- Walk to the left side of a male guest
- Hand each guest a program when they are seated
- Put the aisle runner in place after guests are seated and before the processional begins
- Know the order of seating per tradition such as special guests, grandmothers of the bride and groom, and bride's mother last
- Remove pew ribbons, one row at a time, after the ceremony
- Close windows and check pews for programs or articles left behind after the ceremony
- Are prepared to direct guests to the reception site (having extra maps available, if used)
- Look after elderly relatives or friends
- Participate in garter ceremony, if there is one, and encourage other single men to participate

POST WEDDING

- Coordinate return of rented apparel with head usher or best man

Notes:
____
____
____
____

Groomsmen and Ushers' Checklist

PRE-WEDDING PLANNING PROCESS

- Participate in party for the groom, if there is one
- Pay for own wedding attire and transportation to the wedding
- Contribute to the ushers' gift to the groom. Usually gives an individual gift to the couple expected to attend the rehearsal and the rehearsal dinner

WEDDING DAY

- Review any special seating situations with the head usher before the ceremony begins
- Greets guests as they arrive
- Seat the eldest women first if a group of guests arrive simultaneously
- Ask guests whether they are to be seated on the bride's side or the groom's side
- Offer their right arm to female guests (with the guest's escort walking behind) or ask couples to follow behind (leading couple to their seat)
- Walk to the left side of a male guest
- Hand each guest a program when they are seated
- Put the aisle runner in place after guests are seated and before the processional begins
- Know the order of seating per tradition such as special guests, grandmothers of the bride and groom, and bride's mother last
- Remove pew ribbons, one row at a time, after the ceremony
- Close windows and check pews for programs or articles left behind after the ceremony
- Are prepared to direct guests to the reception site (having extra maps available, if used)
- Look after elderly relatives or friends
- Participate in garter ceremony, if there is one, and encourage other single men to participate

POST WEDDING

- Coordinate return of rented apparel with head usher or best man

Notes:

Groomsmen and Ushers' Checklist

PRE-WEDDING PLANNING PROCESS

- Participate in party for the groom, if there is one
- Pay for own wedding attire and transportation to the wedding
- Contribute to the ushers' gift to the groom. Usually gives an individual gift to the couple expected to attend the rehearsal and the rehearsal dinner

WEDDING DAY

- Review any special seating situations with the head usher before the ceremony begins
- Greets guests as they arrive
- Seat the eldest women first if a group of guests arrive simultaneously
- Ask guests whether they are to be seated on the bride's side or the groom's side
- Offer their right arm to female guests (with the guest's escort walking behind) or ask couples to follow behind (leading couple to their seat)
- Walk to the left side of a male guest
- Hand each guest a program when they are seated
- Put the aisle runner in place after guests are seated and before the processional begins
- Know the order of seating per tradition such as special guests, grandmothers of the bride and groom, and bride's mother last
- Remove pew ribbons, one row at a time, after the ceremony
- Close windows and check pews for programs or articles left behind after the ceremony
- Are prepared to direct guests to the reception site (having extra maps available, if used)
- Look after elderly relatives or friends
- Participate in garter ceremony, if there is one, and encourage other single men to participate

POST WEDDING

- Coordinate return of rented apparel with head usher or best man

Notes:
____
____
____
____

Groomsmen and Ushers' Checklist

PRE-WEDDING PLANNING PROCESS

- Participate in party for the groom, if there is one
- Pay for own wedding attire and transportation to the wedding
- Contribute to the ushers' gift to the groom. Usually gives an individual gift to the couple expected to attend the rehearsal and the rehearsal dinner

WEDDING DAY

- Review any special seating situations with the head usher before the ceremony begins
- Greets guests as they arrive
- Seat the eldest women first if a group of guests arrive simultaneously
- Ask guests whether they are to be seated on the bride's side or the groom's side
- Offer their right arm to female guests (with the guest's escort walking behind) or ask couples to follow behind (leading couple to their seat)
- Walk to the left side of a male guest
- Hand each guest a program when they are seated
- Put the aisle runner in place after guests are seated and before the processional begins
- Know the order of seating per tradition such as special guests, grandmothers of the bride and groom, and bride's mother last
- Remove pew ribbons, one row at a time, after the ceremony
- Close windows and check pews for programs or articles left behind after the ceremony
- Are prepared to direct guests to the reception site (having extra maps available, if used)
- Look after elderly relatives or friends
- Participate in garter ceremony, if there is one, and encourage other single men to participate

POST WEDDING

- Coordinate return of rented apparel with head usher or best man

Notes:
____
____
____

Groomsmen and Ushers' Checklist

PRE-WEDDING PLANNING PROCESS

- Participate in party for the groom, if there is one
- Pay for own wedding attire and transportation to the wedding
- Contribute to the ushers' gift to the groom. Usually gives an individual gift to the couple expected to attend the rehearsal and the rehearsal dinner

WEDDING DAY

- Review any special seating situations with the head usher before the ceremony begins
- Greets guests as they arrive
- Seat the eldest women first if a group of guests arrive simultaneously
- Ask guests whether they are to be seated on the bride's side or the groom's side
- Offer their right arm to female guests (with the guest's escort walking behind) or ask couples to follow behind (leading couple to their seat)
- Walk to the left side of a male guest
- Hand each guest a program when they are seated
- Put the aisle runner in place after guests are seated and before the processional begins
- Know the order of seating per tradition such as special guests, grandmothers of the bride and groom, and bride's mother last
- Remove pew ribbons, one row at a time, after the ceremony
- Close windows and check pews for programs or articles left behind after the ceremony
- Are prepared to direct guests to the reception site (having extra maps available, if used)
- Look after elderly relatives or friends
- Participate in garter ceremony, if there is one, and encourage other single men to participate

POST WEDDING

- Coordinate return of rented apparel with head usher or best man

Notes:
____
____
____
____

Groomsmen and Ushers' Checklist

PRE-WEDDING PLANNING PROCESS

- Participate in party for the groom, if there is one
- Pay for own wedding attire and transportation to the wedding
- Contribute to the ushers' gift to the groom. Usually gives an individual gift to the couple expected to attend the rehearsal and the rehearsal dinner

WEDDING DAY

- Review any special seating situations with the head usher before the ceremony begins
- Greets guests as they arrive
- Seat the eldest women first if a group of guests arrive simultaneously
- Ask guests whether they are to be seated on the bride's side or the groom's side
- Offer their right arm to female guests (with the guest's escort walking behind) or ask couples to follow behind (leading couple to their seat)
- Walk to the left side of a male guest
- Hand each guest a program when they are seated
- Put the aisle runner in place after guests are seated and before the processional begins
- Know the order of seating per tradition such as special guests, grandmothers of the bride and groom, and bride's mother last
- Remove pew ribbons, one row at a time, after the ceremony
- Close windows and check pews for programs or articles left behind after the ceremony
- Are prepared to direct guests to the reception site (having extra maps available, if used)
- Look after elderly relatives or friends
- Participate in garter ceremony, if there is one, and encourage other single men to participate

POST WEDDING

- Coordinate return of rented apparel with head usher or best man

Notes:
____

____

____

____

Groomsmen and Ushers' Checklist

PRE-WEDDING PLANNING PROCESS

- Participate in party for the groom, if there is one
- Pay for own wedding attire and transportation to the wedding
- Contribute to the ushers' gift to the groom. Usually gives an individual gift to the couple expected to attend the rehearsal and the rehearsal dinner

WEDDING DAY

- Review any special seating situations with the head usher before the ceremony begins
- Greets guests as they arrive
- Seat the eldest women first if a group of guests arrive simultaneously
- Ask guests whether they are to be seated on the bride's side or the groom's side
- Offer their right arm to female guests (with the guest's escort walking behind) or ask couples to follow behind (leading couple to their seat)
- Walk to the left side of a male guest
- Hand each guest a program when they are seated
- Put the aisle runner in place after guests are seated and before the processional begins
- Know the order of seating per tradition such as special guests, grandmothers of the bride and groom, and bride's mother last
- Remove pew ribbons, one row at a time, after the ceremony
- Close windows and check pews for programs or articles left behind after the ceremony
- Are prepared to direct guests to the reception site (having extra maps available, if used)
- Look after elderly relatives or friends
- Participate in garter ceremony, if there is one, and encourage other single men to participate

POST WEDDING

- Coordinate return of rented apparel with head usher or best man

Notes:
____
____
____
____

Groomsmen and Ushers' Checklist

PRE-WEDDING PLANNING PROCESS

- Participate in party for the groom, if there is one
- Pay for own wedding attire and transportation to the wedding
- Contribute to the ushers' gift to the groom. Usually gives an individual gift to the couple expected to attend the rehearsal and the rehearsal dinner

WEDDING DAY

- Review any special seating situations with the head usher before the ceremony begins
- Greets guests as they arrive
- Seat the eldest women first if a group of guests arrive simultaneously
- Ask guests whether they are to be seated on the bride's side or the groom's side
- Offer their right arm to female guests (with the guest's escort walking behind) or ask couples to follow behind (leading couple to their seat)
- Walk to the left side of a male guest
- Hand each guest a program when they are seated
- Put the aisle runner in place after guests are seated and before the processional begins
- Know the order of seating per tradition such as special guests, grandmothers of the bride and groom, and bride's mother last
- Remove pew ribbons, one row at a time, after the ceremony
- Close windows and check pews for programs or articles left behind after the ceremony
- Are prepared to direct guests to the reception site (having extra maps available, if used)
- Look after elderly relatives or friends
- Participate in garter ceremony, if there is one, and encourage other single men to participate

POST WEDDING

- Coordinate return of rented apparel with head usher or best man

Notes:

____

____

____

Groomsmen and Ushers' Checklist

PRE-WEDDING PLANNING PROCESS

- Participate in party for the groom, if there is one
- Pay for own wedding attire and transportation to the wedding
- Contribute to the ushers' gift to the groom. Usually gives an individual gift to the couple expected to attend the rehearsal and the rehearsal dinner

WEDDING DAY

- Review any special seating situations with the head usher before the ceremony begins
- Greets guests as they arrive
- Seat the eldest women first if a group of guests arrive simultaneously
- Ask guests whether they are to be seated on the bride's side or the groom's side
- Offer their right arm to female guests (with the guest's escort walking behind) or ask couples to follow behind (leading couple to their seat)
- Walk to the left side of a male guest
- Hand each guest a program when they are seated
- Put the aisle runner in place after guests are seated and before the processional begins
- Know the order of seating per tradition such as special guests, grandmothers of the bride and groom, and bride's mother last
- Remove pew ribbons, one row at a time, after the ceremony
- Close windows and check pews for programs or articles left behind after the ceremony
- Are prepared to direct guests to the reception site (having extra maps available, if used)
- Look after elderly relatives or friends
- Participate in garter ceremony, if there is one, and encourage other single men to participate

POST WEDDING

- Coordinate return of rented apparel with head usher or best man

Notes:
____
____
____
____

Groomsmen and Ushers' Checklist

PRE-WEDDING PLANNING PROCESS

- Participate in party for the groom, if there is one
- Pay for own wedding attire and transportation to the wedding
- Contribute to the ushers' gift to the groom. Usually gives an individual gift to the couple expected to attend the rehearsal and the rehearsal dinner

WEDDING DAY

- Review any special seating situations with the head usher before the ceremony begins
- Greets guests as they arrive
- Seat the eldest women first if a group of guests arrive simultaneously
- Ask guests whether they are to be seated on the bride's side or the groom's side
- Offer their right arm to female guests (with the guest's escort walking behind) or ask couples to follow behind (leading couple to their seat)
- Walk to the left side of a male guest
- Hand each guest a program when they are seated
- Put the aisle runner in place after guests are seated and before the processional begins
- Know the order of seating per tradition such as special guests, grandmothers of the bride and groom, and bride's mother last
- Remove pew ribbons, one row at a time, after the ceremony
- Close windows and check pews for programs or articles left behind after the ceremony
- Are prepared to direct guests to the reception site (having extra maps available, if used)
- Look after elderly relatives or friends
- Participate in garter ceremony, if there is one, and encourage other single men to participate

POST WEDDING

- Coordinate return of rented apparel with head usher or best man

Notes:

Groomsmen and Ushers' Checklist

PRE-WEDDING PLANNING PROCESS

- Participate in party for the groom, if there is one
- Pay for own wedding attire and transportation to the wedding
- Contribute to the ushers' gift to the groom. Usually gives an individual gift to the couple expected to attend the rehearsal and the rehearsal dinner

WEDDING DAY

- Review any special seating situations with the head usher before the ceremony begins
- Greets guests as they arrive
- Seat the eldest women first if a group of guests arrive simultaneously
- Ask guests whether they are to be seated on the bride's side or the groom's side
- Offer their right arm to female guests (with the guest's escort walking behind) or ask couples to follow behind (leading couple to their seat)
- Walk to the left side of a male guest
- Hand each guest a program when they are seated
- Put the aisle runner in place after guests are seated and before the processional begins
- Know the order of seating per tradition such as special guests, grandmothers of the bride and groom, and bride's mother last
- Remove pew ribbons, one row at a time, after the ceremony
- Close windows and check pews for programs or articles left behind after the ceremony
- Are prepared to direct guests to the reception site (having extra maps available, if used)
- Look after elderly relatives or friends
- Participate in garter ceremony, if there is one, and encourage other single men to participate

POST WEDDING

- Coordinate return of rented apparel with head usher or best man

Notes: ____

____

____

____

Groomsmen and Ushers' Checklist

PRE-WEDDING PLANNING PROCESS

- Participate in party for the groom, if there is one
- Pay for own wedding attire and transportation to the wedding
- Contribute to the ushers' gift to the groom. Usually gives an individual gift to the couple expected to attend the rehearsal and the rehearsal dinner

WEDDING DAY

- Review any special seating situations with the head usher before the ceremony begins
- Greets guests as they arrive
- Seat the eldest women first if a group of guests arrive simultaneously
- Ask guests whether they are to be seated on the bride's side or the groom's side
- Offer their right arm to female guests (with the guest's escort walking behind) or ask couples to follow behind (leading couple to their seat)
- Walk to the left side of a male guest
- Hand each guest a program when they are seated
- Put the aisle runner in place after guests are seated and before the processional begins
- Know the order of seating per tradition such as special guests, grandmothers of the bride and groom, and bride's mother last
- Remove pew ribbons, one row at a time, after the ceremony
- Close windows and check pews for programs or articles left behind after the ceremony
- Are prepared to direct guests to the reception site (having extra maps available, if used)
- Look after elderly relatives or friends
- Participate in garter ceremony, if there is one, and encourage other single men to participate

POST WEDDING

- Coordinate return of rented apparel with head usher or best man

Notes:
____
____
____

Groomsmen and Ushers' Checklist

PRE-WEDDING PLANNING PROCESS

- Participate in party for the groom, if there is one
- Pay for own wedding attire and transportation to the wedding
- Contribute to the ushers' gift to the groom. Usually gives an individual gift to the couple expected to attend the rehearsal and the rehearsal dinner

WEDDING DAY

- Review any special seating situations with the head usher before the ceremony begins
- Greets guests as they arrive
- Seat the eldest women first if a group of guests arrive simultaneously
- Ask guests whether they are to be seated on the bride's side or the groom's side
- Offer their right arm to female guests (with the guest's escort walking behind) or ask couples to follow behind (leading couple to their seat)
- Walk to the left side of a male guest
- Hand each guest a program when they are seated
- Put the aisle runner in place after guests are seated and before the processional begins
- Know the order of seating per tradition such as special guests, grandmothers of the bride and groom, and bride's mother last
- Remove pew ribbons, one row at a time, after the ceremony
- Close windows and check pews for programs or articles left behind after the ceremony
- Are prepared to direct guests to the reception site (having extra maps available, if used)
- Look after elderly relatives or friends
- Participate in garter ceremony, if there is one, and encourage other single men to participate

POST WEDDING

- Coordinate return of rented apparel with head usher or best man

Notes:

Groomsmen and Ushers' Checklist

PRE-WEDDING PLANNING PROCESS

- Participate in party for the groom, if there is one
- Pay for own wedding attire and transportation to the wedding
- Contribute to the ushers' gift to the groom. Usually gives an individual gift to the couple expected to attend the rehearsal and the rehearsal dinner

WEDDING DAY

- Review any special seating situations with the head usher before the ceremony begins
- Greets guests as they arrive
- Seat the eldest women first if a group of guests arrive simultaneously
- Ask guests whether they are to be seated on the bride's side or the groom's side
- Offer their right arm to female guests (with the guest's escort walking behind) or ask couples to follow behind (leading couple to their seat)
- Walk to the left side of a male guest
- Hand each guest a program when they are seated
- Put the aisle runner in place after guests are seated and before the processional begins
- Know the order of seating per tradition such as special guests, grandmothers of the bride and groom, and bride's mother last
- Remove pew ribbons, one row at a time, after the ceremony
- Close windows and check pews for programs or articles left behind after the ceremony
- Are prepared to direct guests to the reception site (having extra maps available, if used)
- Look after elderly relatives or friends
- Participate in garter ceremony, if there is one, and encourage other single men to participate

POST WEDDING

- Coordinate return of rented apparel with head usher or best man

Notes:
____
____
____
____

Groomsmen and Ushers' Checklist

PRE-WEDDING PLANNING PROCESS

- Participate in party for the groom, if there is one
- Pay for own wedding attire and transportation to the wedding
- Contribute to the ushers' gift to the groom. Usually gives an individual gift to the couple expected to attend the rehearsal and the rehearsal dinner

WEDDING DAY

- Review any special seating situations with the head usher before the ceremony begins
- Greets guests as they arrive
- Seat the eldest women first if a group of guests arrive simultaneously
- Ask guests whether they are to be seated on the bride's side or the groom's side
- Offer their right arm to female guests (with the guest's escort walking behind) or ask couples to follow behind (leading couple to their seat)
- Walk to the left side of a male guest
- Hand each guest a program when they are seated
- Put the aisle runner in place after guests are seated and before the processional begins
- Know the order of seating per tradition such as special guests, grandmothers of the bride and groom, and bride's mother last
- Remove pew ribbons, one row at a time, after the ceremony
- Close windows and check pews for programs or articles left behind after the ceremony
- Are prepared to direct guests to the reception site (having extra maps available, if used)
- Look after elderly relatives or friends
- Participate in garter ceremony, if there is one, and encourage other single men to participate

POST WEDDING

- Coordinate return of rented apparel with head usher or best man

Notes:
____
____
____
____

Groomsmen and Ushers' Checklist

PRE-WEDDING PLANNING PROCESS

- Participate in party for the groom, if there is one
- Pay for own wedding attire and transportation to the wedding
- Contribute to the ushers' gift to the groom. Usually gives an individual gift to the couple expected to attend the rehearsal and the rehearsal dinner

WEDDING DAY

- Review any special seating situations with the head usher before the ceremony begins
- Greets guests as they arrive
- Seat the eldest women first if a group of guests arrive simultaneously
- Ask guests whether they are to be seated on the bride's side or the groom's side
- Offer their right arm to female guests (with the guest's escort walking behind) or ask couples to follow behind (leading couple to their seat)
- Walk to the left side of a male guest
- Hand each guest a program when they are seated
- Put the aisle runner in place after guests are seated and before the processional begins
- Know the order of seating per tradition such as special guests, grandmothers of the bride and groom, and bride's mother last
- Remove pew ribbons, one row at a time, after the ceremony
- Close windows and check pews for programs or articles left behind after the ceremony
- Are prepared to direct guests to the reception site (having extra maps available, if used)
- Look after elderly relatives or friends
- Participate in garter ceremony, if there is one, and encourage other single men to participate

POST WEDDING

- Coordinate return of rented apparel with head usher or best man

Notes:
____
____
____
____

Groomsmen and Ushers' Checklist

PRE-WEDDING PLANNING PROCESS

- Participate in party for the groom, if there is one
- Pay for own wedding attire and transportation to the wedding
- Contribute to the ushers' gift to the groom. Usually gives an individual gift to the couple expected to attend the rehearsal and the rehearsal dinner

WEDDING DAY

- Review any special seating situations with the head usher before the ceremony begins
- Greets guests as they arrive
- Seat the eldest women first if a group of guests arrive simultaneously
- Ask guests whether they are to be seated on the bride's side or the groom's side
- Offer their right arm to female guests (with the guest's escort walking behind) or ask couples to follow behind (leading couple to their seat)
- Walk to the left side of a male guest
- Hand each guest a program when they are seated
- Put the aisle runner in place after guests are seated and before the processional begins
- Know the order of seating per tradition such as special guests, grandmothers of the bride and groom, and bride's mother last
- Remove pew ribbons, one row at a time, after the ceremony
- Close windows and check pews for programs or articles left behind after the ceremony
- Are prepared to direct guests to the reception site (having extra maps available, if used)
- Look after elderly relatives or friends
- Participate in garter ceremony, if there is one, and encourage other single men to participate

POST WEDDING

- Coordinate return of rented apparel with head usher or best man

Notes:
____
____
____
____

Groomsmen and Ushers' Checklist

PRE-WEDDING PLANNING PROCESS

- Participate in party for the groom, if there is one
- Pay for own wedding attire and transportation to the wedding
- Contribute to the ushers' gift to the groom. Usually gives an individual gift to the couple expected to attend the rehearsal and the rehearsal dinner

WEDDING DAY

- Review any special seating situations with the head usher before the ceremony begins
- Greets guests as they arrive
- Seat the eldest women first if a group of guests arrive simultaneously
- Ask guests whether they are to be seated on the bride's side or the groom's side
- Offer their right arm to female guests (with the guest's escort walking behind) or ask couples to follow behind (leading couple to their seat)
- Walk to the left side of a male guest
- Hand each guest a program when they are seated
- Put the aisle runner in place after guests are seated and before the processional begins
- Know the order of seating per tradition such as special guests, grandmothers of the bride and groom, and bride's mother last
- Remove pew ribbons, one row at a time, after the ceremony
- Close windows and check pews for programs or articles left behind after the ceremony
- Are prepared to direct guests to the reception site (having extra maps available, if used)
- Look after elderly relatives or friends
- Participate in garter ceremony, if there is one, and encourage other single men to participate

POST WEDDING

- Coordinate return of rented apparel with head usher or best man

Notes:
____
____
____
____

Groomsmen and Ushers' Checklist

PRE-WEDDING PLANNING PROCESS

- Participate in party for the groom, if there is one
- Pay for own wedding attire and transportation to the wedding
- Contribute to the ushers' gift to the groom. Usually gives an individual gift to the couple expected to attend the rehearsal and the rehearsal dinner

WEDDING DAY

- Review any special seating situations with the head usher before the ceremony begins
- Greets guests as they arrive
- Seat the eldest women first if a group of guests arrive simultaneously
- Ask guests whether they are to be seated on the bride's side or the groom's side
- Offer their right arm to female guests (with the guest's escort walking behind) or ask couples to follow behind (leading couple to their seat)
- Walk to the left side of a male guest
- Hand each guest a program when they are seated
- Put the aisle runner in place after guests are seated and before the processional begins
- Know the order of seating per tradition such as special guests, grandmothers of the bride and groom, and bride's mother last
- Remove pew ribbons, one row at a time, after the ceremony
- Close windows and check pews for programs or articles left behind after the ceremony
- Are prepared to direct guests to the reception site (having extra maps available, if used)
- Look after elderly relatives or friends
- Participate in garter ceremony, if there is one, and encourage other single men to participate

POST WEDDING

- Coordinate return of rented apparel with head usher or best man

Notes:
____
____
____
____

Groomsmen and Ushers' Checklist

PRE-WEDDING PLANNING PROCESS

- Participate in party for the groom, if there is one
- Pay for own wedding attire and transportation to the wedding
- Contribute to the ushers' gift to the groom. Usually gives an individual gift to the couple expected to attend the rehearsal and the rehearsal dinner

WEDDING DAY

- Review any special seating situations with the head usher before the ceremony begins
- Greets guests as they arrive
- Seat the eldest women first if a group of guests arrive simultaneously
- Ask guests whether they are to be seated on the bride's side or the groom's side
- Offer their right arm to female guests (with the guest's escort walking behind) or ask couples to follow behind (leading couple to their seat)
- Walk to the left side of a male guest
- Hand each guest a program when they are seated
- Put the aisle runner in place after guests are seated and before the processional begins
- Know the order of seating per tradition such as special guests, grandmothers of the bride and groom, and bride's mother last
- Remove pew ribbons, one row at a time, after the ceremony
- Close windows and check pews for programs or articles left behind after the ceremony
- Are prepared to direct guests to the reception site (having extra maps available, if used)
- Look after elderly relatives or friends
- Participate in garter ceremony, if there is one, and encourage other single men to participate

POST WEDDING

- Coordinate return of rented apparel with head usher or best man

Notes:
____
____
____
____

Groomsmen and Ushers' Checklist

PRE-WEDDING PLANNING PROCESS

- Participate in party for the groom, if there is one
- Pay for own wedding attire and transportation to the wedding
- Contribute to the ushers' gift to the groom. Usually gives an individual gift to the couple expected to attend the rehearsal and the rehearsal dinner

WEDDING DAY

- Review any special seating situations with the head usher before the ceremony begins
- Greets guests as they arrive
- Seat the eldest women first if a group of guests arrive simultaneously
- Ask guests whether they are to be seated on the bride's side or the groom's side
- Offer their right arm to female guests (with the guest's escort walking behind) or ask couples to follow behind (leading couple to their seat)
- Walk to the left side of a male guest
- Hand each guest a program when they are seated
- Put the aisle runner in place after guests are seated and before the processional begins
- Know the order of seating per tradition such as special guests, grandmothers of the bride and groom, and bride's mother last
- Remove pew ribbons, one row at a time, after the ceremony
- Close windows and check pews for programs or articles left behind after the ceremony
- Are prepared to direct guests to the reception site (having extra maps available, if used)
- Look after elderly relatives or friends
- Participate in garter ceremony, if there is one, and encourage other single men to participate

POST WEDDING

- Coordinate return of rented apparel with head usher or best man

Notes:

Groomsmen and Ushers' Checklist

PRE-WEDDING PLANNING PROCESS

- Participate in party for the groom, if there is one
- Pay for own wedding attire and transportation to the wedding
- Contribute to the ushers' gift to the groom. Usually gives an individual gift to the couple expected to attend the rehearsal and the rehearsal dinner

WEDDING DAY

- Review any special seating situations with the head usher before the ceremony begins
- Greets guests as they arrive
- Seat the eldest women first if a group of guests arrive simultaneously
- Ask guests whether they are to be seated on the bride's side or the groom's side
- Offer their right arm to female guests (with the guest's escort walking behind) or ask couples to follow behind (leading couple to their seat)
- Walk to the left side of a male guest
- Hand each guest a program when they are seated
- Put the aisle runner in place after guests are seated and before the processional begins
- Know the order of seating per tradition such as special guests, grandmothers of the bride and groom, and bride's mother last
- Remove pew ribbons, one row at a time, after the ceremony
- Close windows and check pews for programs or articles left behind after the ceremony
- Are prepared to direct guests to the reception site (having extra maps available, if used)
- Look after elderly relatives or friends
- Participate in garter ceremony, if there is one, and encourage other single men to participate

POST WEDDING

- Coordinate return of rented apparel with head usher or best man

Notes:
____
____
____
____

Groomsmen and Ushers' Checklist

PRE-WEDDING PLANNING PROCESS

- Participate in party for the groom, if there is one
- Pay for own wedding attire and transportation to the wedding
- Contribute to the ushers' gift to the groom. Usually gives an individual gift to the couple expected to attend the rehearsal and the rehearsal dinner

WEDDING DAY

- Review any special seating situations with the head usher before the ceremony begins
- Greets guests as they arrive
- Seat the eldest women first if a group of guests arrive simultaneously
- Ask guests whether they are to be seated on the bride's side or the groom's side
- Offer their right arm to female guests (with the guest's escort walking behind) or ask couples to follow behind (leading couple to their seat)
- Walk to the left side of a male guest
- Hand each guest a program when they are seated
- Put the aisle runner in place after guests are seated and before the processional begins
- Know the order of seating per tradition such as special guests, grandmothers of the bride and groom, and bride's mother last
- Remove pew ribbons, one row at a time, after the ceremony
- Close windows and check pews for programs or articles left behind after the ceremony
- Are prepared to direct guests to the reception site (having extra maps available, if used)
- Look after elderly relatives or friends
- Participate in garter ceremony, if there is one, and encourage other single men to participate

POST WEDDING

- Coordinate return of rented apparel with head usher or best man

Notes:
____
____
____
____

Groomsmen and Ushers' Checklist

PRE-WEDDING PLANNING PROCESS

- Participate in party for the groom, if there is one
- Pay for own wedding attire and transportation to the wedding
- Contribute to the ushers' gift to the groom. Usually gives an individual gift to the couple expected to attend the rehearsal and the rehearsal dinner

WEDDING DAY

- Review any special seating situations with the head usher before the ceremony begins
- Greets guests as they arrive
- Seat the eldest women first if a group of guests arrive simultaneously
- Ask guests whether they are to be seated on the bride's side or the groom's side
- Offer their right arm to female guests (with the guest's escort walking behind) or ask couples to follow behind (leading couple to their seat)
- Walk to the left side of a male guest
- Hand each guest a program when they are seated
- Put the aisle runner in place after guests are seated and before the processional begins
- Know the order of seating per tradition such as special guests, grandmothers of the bride and groom, and bride's mother last
- Remove pew ribbons, one row at a time, after the ceremony
- Close windows and check pews for programs or articles left behind after the ceremony
- Are prepared to direct guests to the reception site (having extra maps available, if used)
- Look after elderly relatives or friends
- Participate in garter ceremony, if there is one, and encourage other single men to participate

POST WEDDING

- Coordinate return of rented apparel with head usher or best man

Notes: ____

____

____

____

Groomsmen and Ushers' Checklist

PRE-WEDDING PLANNING PROCESS

- Participate in party for the groom, if there is one
- Pay for own wedding attire and transportation to the wedding
- Contribute to the ushers' gift to the groom. Usually gives an individual gift to the couple expected to attend the rehearsal and the rehearsal dinner

WEDDING DAY

- Review any special seating situations with the head usher before the ceremony begins
- Greets guests as they arrive
- Seat the eldest women first if a group of guests arrive simultaneously
- Ask guests whether they are to be seated on the bride's side or the groom's side
- Offer their right arm to female guests (with the guest's escort walking behind) or ask couples to follow behind (leading couple to their seat)
- Walk to the left side of a male guest
- Hand each guest a program when they are seated
- Put the aisle runner in place after guests are seated and before the processional begins
- Know the order of seating per tradition such as special guests, grandmothers of the bride and groom, and bride's mother last
- Remove pew ribbons, one row at a time, after the ceremony
- Close windows and check pews for programs or articles left behind after the ceremony
- Are prepared to direct guests to the reception site (having extra maps available, if used)
- Look after elderly relatives or friends
- Participate in garter ceremony, if there is one, and encourage other single men to participate

POST WEDDING

- Coordinate return of rented apparel with head usher or best man

Notes:
____
____
____
____

Groomsmen and Ushers' Checklist

PRE-WEDDING PLANNING PROCESS

- Participate in party for the groom, if there is one
- Pay for own wedding attire and transportation to the wedding
- Contribute to the ushers' gift to the groom. Usually gives an individual gift to the couple expected to attend the rehearsal and the rehearsal dinner

WEDDING DAY

- Review any special seating situations with the head usher before the ceremony begins
- Greets guests as they arrive
- Seat the eldest women first if a group of guests arrive simultaneously
- Ask guests whether they are to be seated on the bride's side or the groom's side
- Offer their right arm to female guests (with the guest's escort walking behind) or ask couples to follow behind (leading couple to their seat)
- Walk to the left side of a male guest
- Hand each guest a program when they are seated
- Put the aisle runner in place after guests are seated and before the processional begins
- Know the order of seating per tradition such as special guests, grandmothers of the bride and groom, and bride's mother last
- Remove pew ribbons, one row at a time, after the ceremony
- Close windows and check pews for programs or articles left behind after the ceremony
- Are prepared to direct guests to the reception site (having extra maps available, if used)
- Look after elderly relatives or friends
- Participate in garter ceremony, if there is one, and encourage other single men to participate

POST WEDDING

- Coordinate return of rented apparel with head usher or best man

Notes:
____
____
____
____

Groomsmen and Ushers' Checklist

PRE-WEDDING PLANNING PROCESS

- Participate in party for the groom, if there is one
- Pay for own wedding attire and transportation to the wedding
- Contribute to the ushers' gift to the groom. Usually gives an individual gift to the couple expected to attend the rehearsal and the rehearsal dinner

WEDDING DAY

- Review any special seating situations with the head usher before the ceremony begins
- Greets guests as they arrive
- Seat the eldest women first if a group of guests arrive simultaneously
- Ask guests whether they are to be seated on the bride's side or the groom's side
- Offer their right arm to female guests (with the guest's escort walking behind) or ask couples to follow behind (leading couple to their seat)
- Walk to the left side of a male guest
- Hand each guest a program when they are seated
- Put the aisle runner in place after guests are seated and before the processional begins
- Know the order of seating per tradition such as special guests, grandmothers of the bride and groom, and bride's mother last
- Remove pew ribbons, one row at a time, after the ceremony
- Close windows and check pews for programs or articles left behind after the ceremony
- Are prepared to direct guests to the reception site (having extra maps available, if used)
- Look after elderly relatives or friends
- Participate in garter ceremony, if there is one, and encourage other single men to participate

POST WEDDING

- Coordinate return of rented apparel with head usher or best man

Notes: ____

____

____

____

Groomsmen and Ushers' Checklist

PRE-WEDDING PLANNING PROCESS

- Participate in party for the groom, if there is one
- Pay for own wedding attire and transportation to the wedding
- Contribute to the ushers' gift to the groom. Usually gives an individual gift to the couple expected to attend the rehearsal and the rehearsal dinner

WEDDING DAY

- Review any special seating situations with the head usher before the ceremony begins
- Greets guests as they arrive
- Seat the eldest women first if a group of guests arrive simultaneously
- Ask guests whether they are to be seated on the bride's side or the groom's side
- Offer their right arm to female guests (with the guest's escort walking behind) or ask couples to follow behind (leading couple to their seat)
- Walk to the left side of a male guest
- Hand each guest a program when they are seated
- Put the aisle runner in place after guests are seated and before the processional begins
- Know the order of seating per tradition such as special guests, grandmothers of the bride and groom, and bride's mother last
- Remove pew ribbons, one row at a time, after the ceremony
- Close windows and check pews for programs or articles left behind after the ceremony
- Are prepared to direct guests to the reception site (having extra maps available, if used)
- Look after elderly relatives or friends
- Participate in garter ceremony, if there is one, and encourage other single men to participate

POST WEDDING

- Coordinate return of rented apparel with head usher or best man

Notes:
____
____
____
____

Groomsmen and Ushers' Checklist

PRE-WEDDING PLANNING PROCESS

- Participate in party for the groom, if there is one
- Pay for own wedding attire and transportation to the wedding
- Contribute to the ushers' gift to the groom. Usually gives an individual gift to the couple expected to attend the rehearsal and the rehearsal dinner

WEDDING DAY

- Review any special seating situations with the head usher before the ceremony begins
- Greets guests as they arrive
- Seat the eldest women first if a group of guests arrive simultaneously
- Ask guests whether they are to be seated on the bride's side or the groom's side
- Offer their right arm to female guests (with the guest's escort walking behind) or ask couples to follow behind (leading couple to their seat)
- Walk to the left side of a male guest
- Hand each guest a program when they are seated
- Put the aisle runner in place after guests are seated and before the processional begins
- Know the order of seating per tradition such as special guests, grandmothers of the bride and groom, and bride's mother last
- Remove pew ribbons, one row at a time, after the ceremony
- Close windows and check pews for programs or articles left behind after the ceremony
- Are prepared to direct guests to the reception site (having extra maps available, if used)
- Look after elderly relatives or friends
- Participate in garter ceremony, if there is one, and encourage other single men to participate

POST WEDDING

- Coordinate return of rented apparel with head usher or best man

Notes:

Groomsmen and Ushers' Checklist

PRE-WEDDING PLANNING PROCESS

- Participate in party for the groom, if there is one
- Pay for own wedding attire and transportation to the wedding
- Contribute to the ushers' gift to the groom. Usually gives an individual gift to the couple expected to attend the rehearsal and the rehearsal dinner

WEDDING DAY

- Review any special seating situations with the head usher before the ceremony begins
- Greets guests as they arrive
- Seat the eldest women first if a group of guests arrive simultaneously
- Ask guests whether they are to be seated on the bride's side or the groom's side
- Offer their right arm to female guests (with the guest's escort walking behind) or ask couples to follow behind (leading couple to their seat)
- Walk to the left side of a male guest
- Hand each guest a program when they are seated
- Put the aisle runner in place after guests are seated and before the processional begins
- Know the order of seating per tradition such as special guests, grandmothers of the bride and groom, and bride's mother last
- Remove pew ribbons, one row at a time, after the ceremony
- Close windows and check pews for programs or articles left behind after the ceremony
- Are prepared to direct guests to the reception site (having extra maps available, if used)
- Look after elderly relatives or friends
- Participate in garter ceremony, if there is one, and encourage other single men to participate

POST WEDDING

- Coordinate return of rented apparel with head usher or best man

Notes:

Groomsmen and Ushers' Checklist

PRE-WEDDING PLANNING PROCESS

- Participate in party for the groom, if there is one
- Pay for own wedding attire and transportation to the wedding
- Contribute to the ushers' gift to the groom. Usually gives an individual gift to the couple expected to attend the rehearsal and the rehearsal dinner

WEDDING DAY

- Review any special seating situations with the head usher before the ceremony begins
- Greets guests as they arrive
- Seat the eldest women first if a group of guests arrive simultaneously
- Ask guests whether they are to be seated on the bride's side or the groom's side
- Offer their right arm to female guests (with the guest's escort walking behind) or ask couples to follow behind (leading couple to their seat)
- Walk to the left side of a male guest
- Hand each guest a program when they are seated
- Put the aisle runner in place after guests are seated and before the processional begins
- Know the order of seating per tradition such as special guests, grandmothers of the bride and groom, and bride's mother last
- Remove pew ribbons, one row at a time, after the ceremony
- Close windows and check pews for programs or articles left behind after the ceremony
- Are prepared to direct guests to the reception site (having extra maps available, if used)
- Look after elderly relatives or friends
- Participate in garter ceremony, if there is one, and encourage other single men to participate

POST WEDDING

- Coordinate return of rented apparel with head usher or best man

Notes: ____

____

____

____

Groomsmen and Ushers' Checklist

PRE-WEDDING PLANNING PROCESS

- Participate in party for the groom, if there is one
- Pay for own wedding attire and transportation to the wedding
- Contribute to the ushers' gift to the groom. Usually gives an individual gift to the couple expected to attend the rehearsal and the rehearsal dinner

WEDDING DAY

- Review any special seating situations with the head usher before the ceremony begins
- Greets guests as they arrive
- Seat the eldest women first if a group of guests arrive simultaneously
- Ask guests whether they are to be seated on the bride's side or the groom's side
- Offer their right arm to female guests (with the guest's escort walking behind) or ask couples to follow behind (leading couple to their seat)
- Walk to the left side of a male guest
- Hand each guest a program when they are seated
- Put the aisle runner in place after guests are seated and before the processional begins
- Know the order of seating per tradition such as special guests, grandmothers of the bride and groom, and bride's mother last
- Remove pew ribbons, one row at a time, after the ceremony
- Close windows and check pews for programs or articles left behind after the ceremony
- Are prepared to direct guests to the reception site (having extra maps available, if used)
- Look after elderly relatives or friends
- Participate in garter ceremony, if there is one, and encourage other single men to participate

POST WEDDING

- Coordinate return of rented apparel with head usher or best man

Notes:
____
____
____
____

Groomsmen and Ushers' Checklist

PRE-WEDDING PLANNING PROCESS

- Participate in party for the groom, if there is one
- Pay for own wedding attire and transportation to the wedding
- Contribute to the ushers' gift to the groom. Usually gives an individual gift to the couple expected to attend the rehearsal and the rehearsal dinner

WEDDING DAY

- Review any special seating situations with the head usher before the ceremony begins
- Greets guests as they arrive
- Seat the eldest women first if a group of guests arrive simultaneously
- Ask guests whether they are to be seated on the bride's side or the groom's side
- Offer their right arm to female guests (with the guest's escort walking behind) or ask couples to follow behind (leading couple to their seat)
- Walk to the left side of a male guest
- Hand each guest a program when they are seated
- Put the aisle runner in place after guests are seated and before the processional begins
- Know the order of seating per tradition such as special guests, grandmothers of the bride and groom, and bride's mother last
- Remove pew ribbons, one row at a time, after the ceremony
- Close windows and check pews for programs or articles left behind after the ceremony
- Are prepared to direct guests to the reception site (having extra maps available, if used)
- Look after elderly relatives or friends
- Participate in garter ceremony, if there is one, and encourage other single men to participate

POST WEDDING

- Coordinate return of rented apparel with head usher or best man

Notes: ____

____

____

____

Groomsmen and Ushers' Checklist

PRE-WEDDING PLANNING PROCESS

- Participate in party for the groom, if there is one
- Pay for own wedding attire and transportation to the wedding
- Contribute to the ushers' gift to the groom. Usually gives an individual gift to the couple expected to attend the rehearsal and the rehearsal dinner

WEDDING DAY

- Review any special seating situations with the head usher before the ceremony begins
- Greets guests as they arrive
- Seat the eldest women first if a group of guests arrive simultaneously
- Ask guests whether they are to be seated on the bride's side or the groom's side
- Offer their right arm to female guests (with the guest's escort walking behind) or ask couples to follow behind (leading couple to their seat)
- Walk to the left side of a male guest
- Hand each guest a program when they are seated
- Put the aisle runner in place after guests are seated and before the processional begins
- Know the order of seating per tradition such as special guests, grandmothers of the bride and groom, and bride's mother last
- Remove pew ribbons, one row at a time, after the ceremony
- Close windows and check pews for programs or articles left behind after the ceremony
- Are prepared to direct guests to the reception site (having extra maps available, if used)
- Look after elderly relatives or friends
- Participate in garter ceremony, if there is one, and encourage other single men to participate

POST WEDDING

- Coordinate return of rented apparel with head usher or best man

Notes:

Groomsmen and Ushers' Checklist

PRE-WEDDING PLANNING PROCESS

- Participate in party for the groom, if there is one
- Pay for own wedding attire and transportation to the wedding
- Contribute to the ushers' gift to the groom. Usually gives an individual gift to the couple expected to attend the rehearsal and the rehearsal dinner

WEDDING DAY

- Review any special seating situations with the head usher before the ceremony begins
- Greets guests as they arrive
- Seat the eldest women first if a group of guests arrive simultaneously
- Ask guests whether they are to be seated on the bride's side or the groom's side
- Offer their right arm to female guests (with the guest's escort walking behind) or ask couples to follow behind (leading couple to their seat)
- Walk to the left side of a male guest
- Hand each guest a program when they are seated
- Put the aisle runner in place after guests are seated and before the processional begins
- Know the order of seating per tradition such as special guests, grandmothers of the bride and groom, and bride's mother last
- Remove pew ribbons, one row at a time, after the ceremony
- Close windows and check pews for programs or articles left behind after the ceremony
- Are prepared to direct guests to the reception site (having extra maps available, if used)
- Look after elderly relatives or friends
- Participate in garter ceremony, if there is one, and encourage other single men to participate

POST WEDDING

- Coordinate return of rented apparel with head usher or best man

Notes:
____
____
____
____

Groomsmen and Ushers' Checklist

PRE-WEDDING PLANNING PROCESS

- Participate in party for the groom, if there is one
- Pay for own wedding attire and transportation to the wedding
- Contribute to the ushers' gift to the groom. Usually gives an individual gift to the couple expected to attend the rehearsal and the rehearsal dinner

WEDDING DAY

- Review any special seating situations with the head usher before the ceremony begins
- Greets guests as they arrive
- Seat the eldest women first if a group of guests arrive simultaneously
- Ask guests whether they are to be seated on the bride's side or the groom's side
- Offer their right arm to female guests (with the guest's escort walking behind) or ask couples to follow behind (leading couple to their seat)
- Walk to the left side of a male guest
- Hand each guest a program when they are seated
- Put the aisle runner in place after guests are seated and before the processional begins
- Know the order of seating per tradition such as special guests, grandmothers of the bride and groom, and bride's mother last
- Remove pew ribbons, one row at a time, after the ceremony
- Close windows and check pews for programs or articles left behind after the ceremony
- Are prepared to direct guests to the reception site (having extra maps available, if used)
- Look after elderly relatives or friends
- Participate in garter ceremony, if there is one, and encourage other single men to participate

POST WEDDING

- Coordinate return of rented apparel with head usher or best man

Notes:
____
____
____
____

Groomsmen and Ushers' Checklist

PRE-WEDDING PLANNING PROCESS

- Participate in party for the groom, if there is one
- Pay for own wedding attire and transportation to the wedding
- Contribute to the ushers' gift to the groom. Usually gives an individual gift to the couple expected to attend the rehearsal and the rehearsal dinner

WEDDING DAY

- Review any special seating situations with the head usher before the ceremony begins
- Greets guests as they arrive
- Seat the eldest women first if a group of guests arrive simultaneously
- Ask guests whether they are to be seated on the bride's side or the groom's side
- Offer their right arm to female guests (with the guest's escort walking behind) or ask couples to follow behind (leading couple to their seat)
- Walk to the left side of a male guest
- Hand each guest a program when they are seated
- Put the aisle runner in place after guests are seated and before the processional begins
- Know the order of seating per tradition such as special guests, grandmothers of the bride and groom, and bride's mother last
- Remove pew ribbons, one row at a time, after the ceremony
- Close windows and check pews for programs or articles left behind after the ceremony
- Are prepared to direct guests to the reception site (having extra maps available, if used)
- Look after elderly relatives or friends
- Participate in garter ceremony, if there is one, and encourage other single men to participate

POST WEDDING

- Coordinate return of rented apparel with head usher or best man

Notes:
____
____
____
____

Groomsmen and Ushers' Checklist

PRE-WEDDING PLANNING PROCESS

- Participate in party for the groom, if there is one
- Pay for own wedding attire and transportation to the wedding
- Contribute to the ushers' gift to the groom. Usually gives an individual gift to the couple expected to attend the rehearsal and the rehearsal dinner

WEDDING DAY

- Review any special seating situations with the head usher before the ceremony begins
- Greets guests as they arrive
- Seat the eldest women first if a group of guests arrive simultaneously
- Ask guests whether they are to be seated on the bride's side or the groom's side
- Offer their right arm to female guests (with the guest's escort walking behind) or ask couples to follow behind (leading couple to their seat)
- Walk to the left side of a male guest
- Hand each guest a program when they are seated
- Put the aisle runner in place after guests are seated and before the processional begins
- Know the order of seating per tradition such as special guests, grandmothers of the bride and groom, and bride's mother last
- Remove pew ribbons, one row at a time, after the ceremony
- Close windows and check pews for programs or articles left behind after the ceremony
- Are prepared to direct guests to the reception site (having extra maps available, if used)
- Look after elderly relatives or friends
- Participate in garter ceremony, if there is one, and encourage other single men to participate

POST WEDDING

- Coordinate return of rented apparel with head usher or best man

Notes:
____
____
____
____

Groomsmen and Ushers' Checklist

PRE-WEDDING PLANNING PROCESS

- Participate in party for the groom, if there is one
- Pay for own wedding attire and transportation to the wedding
- Contribute to the ushers' gift to the groom. Usually gives an individual gift to the couple expected to attend the rehearsal and the rehearsal dinner

WEDDING DAY

- Review any special seating situations with the head usher before the ceremony begins
- Greets guests as they arrive
- Seat the eldest women first if a group of guests arrive simultaneously
- Ask guests whether they are to be seated on the bride's side or the groom's side
- Offer their right arm to female guests (with the guest's escort walking behind) or ask couples to follow behind (leading couple to their seat)
- Walk to the left side of a male guest
- Hand each guest a program when they are seated
- Put the aisle runner in place after guests are seated and before the processional begins
- Know the order of seating per tradition such as special guests, grandmothers of the bride and groom, and bride's mother last
- Remove pew ribbons, one row at a time, after the ceremony
- Close windows and check pews for programs or articles left behind after the ceremony
- Are prepared to direct guests to the reception site (having extra maps available, if used)
- Look after elderly relatives or friends
- Participate in garter ceremony, if there is one, and encourage other single men to participate

POST WEDDING

- Coordinate return of rented apparel with head usher or best man

Notes: ____

____

____

____

Groomsmen and Ushers' Checklist

PRE-WEDDING PLANNING PROCESS

- Participate in party for the groom, if there is one
- Pay for own wedding attire and transportation to the wedding
- Contribute to the ushers' gift to the groom. Usually gives an individual gift to the couple expected to attend the rehearsal and the rehearsal dinner

WEDDING DAY

- Review any special seating situations with the head usher before the ceremony begins
- Greets guests as they arrive
- Seat the eldest women first if a group of guests arrive simultaneously
- Ask guests whether they are to be seated on the bride's side or the groom's side
- Offer their right arm to female guests (with the guest's escort walking behind) or ask couples to follow behind (leading couple to their seat)
- Walk to the left side of a male guest
- Hand each guest a program when they are seated
- Put the aisle runner in place after guests are seated and before the processional begins
- Know the order of seating per tradition such as special guests, grandmothers of the bride and groom, and bride's mother last
- Remove pew ribbons, one row at a time, after the ceremony
- Close windows and check pews for programs or articles left behind after the ceremony
- Are prepared to direct guests to the reception site (having extra maps available, if used)
- Look after elderly relatives or friends
- Participate in garter ceremony, if there is one, and encourage other single men to participate

POST WEDDING

- Coordinate return of rented apparel with head usher or best man

Notes:

Groomsmen and Ushers' Checklist

PRE-WEDDING PLANNING PROCESS

- Participate in party for the groom, if there is one
- Pay for own wedding attire and transportation to the wedding
- Contribute to the ushers' gift to the groom. Usually gives an individual gift to the couple expected to attend the rehearsal and the rehearsal dinner

WEDDING DAY

- Review any special seating situations with the head usher before the ceremony begins
- Greets guests as they arrive
- Seat the eldest women first if a group of guests arrive simultaneously
- Ask guests whether they are to be seated on the bride's side or the groom's side
- Offer their right arm to female guests (with the guest's escort walking behind) or ask couples to follow behind (leading couple to their seat)
- Walk to the left side of a male guest
- Hand each guest a program when they are seated
- Put the aisle runner in place after guests are seated and before the processional begins
- Know the order of seating per tradition such as special guests, grandmothers of the bride and groom, and bride's mother last
- Remove pew ribbons, one row at a time, after the ceremony
- Close windows and check pews for programs or articles left behind after the ceremony
- Are prepared to direct guests to the reception site (having extra maps available, if used)
- Look after elderly relatives or friends
- Participate in garter ceremony, if there is one, and encourage other single men to participate

POST WEDDING

- Coordinate return of rented apparel with head usher or best man

Notes:
____
____
____
____

Groomsmen and Ushers' Checklist

PRE-WEDDING PLANNING PROCESS

- Participate in party for the groom, if there is one
- Pay for own wedding attire and transportation to the wedding
- Contribute to the ushers' gift to the groom. Usually gives an individual gift to the couple expected to attend the rehearsal and the rehearsal dinner

WEDDING DAY

- Review any special seating situations with the head usher before the ceremony begins
- Greets guests as they arrive
- Seat the eldest women first if a group of guests arrive simultaneously
- Ask guests whether they are to be seated on the bride's side or the groom's side
- Offer their right arm to female guests (with the guest's escort walking behind) or ask couples to follow behind (leading couple to their seat)
- Walk to the left side of a male guest
- Hand each guest a program when they are seated
- Put the aisle runner in place after guests are seated and before the processional begins
- Know the order of seating per tradition such as special guests, grandmothers of the bride and groom, and bride's mother last
- Remove pew ribbons, one row at a time, after the ceremony
- Close windows and check pews for programs or articles left behind after the ceremony
- Are prepared to direct guests to the reception site (having extra maps available, if used)
- Look after elderly relatives or friends
- Participate in garter ceremony, if there is one, and encourage other single men to participate

POST WEDDING

- Coordinate return of rented apparel with head usher or best man

Notes:

Groomsmen and Ushers' Checklist

PRE-WEDDING PLANNING PROCESS

- Participate in party for the groom, if there is one
- Pay for own wedding attire and transportation to the wedding
- Contribute to the ushers' gift to the groom. Usually gives an individual gift to the couple expected to attend the rehearsal and the rehearsal dinner

WEDDING DAY

- Review any special seating situations with the head usher before the ceremony begins
- Greets guests as they arrive
- Seat the eldest women first if a group of guests arrive simultaneously
- Ask guests whether they are to be seated on the bride's side or the groom's side
- Offer their right arm to female guests (with the guest's escort walking behind) or ask couples to follow behind (leading couple to their seat)
- Walk to the left side of a male guest
- Hand each guest a program when they are seated
- Put the aisle runner in place after guests are seated and before the processional begins
- Know the order of seating per tradition such as special guests, grandmothers of the bride and groom, and bride's mother last
- Remove pew ribbons, one row at a time, after the ceremony
- Close windows and check pews for programs or articles left behind after the ceremony
- Are prepared to direct guests to the reception site (having extra maps available, if used)
- Look after elderly relatives or friends
- Participate in garter ceremony, if there is one, and encourage other single men to participate

POST WEDDING

- Coordinate return of rented apparel with head usher or best man

Notes: ____

____

____

____

Groomsmen and Ushers' Checklist

PRE-WEDDING PLANNING PROCESS

- Participate in party for the groom, if there is one
- Pay for own wedding attire and transportation to the wedding
- Contribute to the ushers' gift to the groom. Usually gives an individual gift to the couple expected to attend the rehearsal and the rehearsal dinner

WEDDING DAY

- Review any special seating situations with the head usher before the ceremony begins
- Greets guests as they arrive
- Seat the eldest women first if a group of guests arrive simultaneously
- Ask guests whether they are to be seated on the bride's side or the groom's side
- Offer their right arm to female guests (with the guest's escort walking behind) or ask couples to follow behind (leading couple to their seat)
- Walk to the left side of a male guest
- Hand each guest a program when they are seated
- Put the aisle runner in place after guests are seated and before the processional begins
- Know the order of seating per tradition such as special guests, grandmothers of the bride and groom, and bride's mother last
- Remove pew ribbons, one row at a time, after the ceremony
- Close windows and check pews for programs or articles left behind after the ceremony
- Are prepared to direct guests to the reception site (having extra maps available, if used)
- Look after elderly relatives or friends
- Participate in garter ceremony, if there is one, and encourage other single men to participate

POST WEDDING

- Coordinate return of rented apparel with head usher or best man

Notes:
____
____
____
____

Groomsmen and Ushers' Checklist

PRE-WEDDING PLANNING PROCESS

- Participate in party for the groom, if there is one
- Pay for own wedding attire and transportation to the wedding
- Contribute to the ushers' gift to the groom. Usually gives an individual gift to the couple expected to attend the rehearsal and the rehearsal dinner

WEDDING DAY

- Review any special seating situations with the head usher before the ceremony begins
- Greets guests as they arrive
- Seat the eldest women first if a group of guests arrive simultaneously
- Ask guests whether they are to be seated on the bride's side or the groom's side
- Offer their right arm to female guests (with the guest's escort walking behind) or ask couples to follow behind (leading couple to their seat)
- Walk to the left side of a male guest
- Hand each guest a program when they are seated
- Put the aisle runner in place after guests are seated and before the processional begins
- Know the order of seating per tradition such as special guests, grandmothers of the bride and groom, and bride's mother last
- Remove pew ribbons, one row at a time, after the ceremony
- Close windows and check pews for programs or articles left behind after the ceremony
- Are prepared to direct guests to the reception site (having extra maps available, if used)
- Look after elderly relatives or friends
- Participate in garter ceremony, if there is one, and encourage other single men to participate

POST WEDDING

- Coordinate return of rented apparel with head usher or best man

Notes:
____
____
____
____

Groomsmen and Ushers' Checklist

PRE-WEDDING PLANNING PROCESS

- Participate in party for the groom, if there is one
- Pay for own wedding attire and transportation to the wedding
- Contribute to the ushers' gift to the groom. Usually gives an individual gift to the couple expected to attend the rehearsal and the rehearsal dinner

WEDDING DAY

- Review any special seating situations with the head usher before the ceremony begins
- Greets guests as they arrive
- Seat the eldest women first if a group of guests arrive simultaneously
- Ask guests whether they are to be seated on the bride's side or the groom's side
- Offer their right arm to female guests (with the guest's escort walking behind) or ask couples to follow behind (leading couple to their seat)
- Walk to the left side of a male guest
- Hand each guest a program when they are seated
- Put the aisle runner in place after guests are seated and before the processional begins
- Know the order of seating per tradition such as special guests, grandmothers of the bride and groom, and bride's mother last
- Remove pew ribbons, one row at a time, after the ceremony
- Close windows and check pews for programs or articles left behind after the ceremony
- Are prepared to direct guests to the reception site (having extra maps available, if used)
- Look after elderly relatives or friends
- Participate in garter ceremony, if there is one, and encourage other single men to participate

POST WEDDING

- Coordinate return of rented apparel with head usher or best man

Notes:
____
____
____
____

Groomsmen and Ushers' Checklist

PRE-WEDDING PLANNING PROCESS

- Participate in party for the groom, if there is one
- Pay for own wedding attire and transportation to the wedding
- Contribute to the ushers' gift to the groom. Usually gives an individual gift to the couple expected to attend the rehearsal and the rehearsal dinner

WEDDING DAY

- Review any special seating situations with the head usher before the ceremony begins
- Greets guests as they arrive
- Seat the eldest women first if a group of guests arrive simultaneously
- Ask guests whether they are to be seated on the bride's side or the groom's side
- Offer their right arm to female guests (with the guest's escort walking behind) or ask couples to follow behind (leading couple to their seat)
- Walk to the left side of a male guest
- Hand each guest a program when they are seated
- Put the aisle runner in place after guests are seated and before the processional begins
- Know the order of seating per tradition such as special guests, grandmothers of the bride and groom, and bride's mother last
- Remove pew ribbons, one row at a time, after the ceremony
- Close windows and check pews for programs or articles left behind after the ceremony
- Are prepared to direct guests to the reception site (having extra maps available, if used)
- Look after elderly relatives or friends
- Participate in garter ceremony, if there is one, and encourage other single men to participate

POST WEDDING

- Coordinate return of rented apparel with head usher or best man

Notes: ____

____

____

____

Groomsmen and Ushers' Checklist

PRE-WEDDING PLANNING PROCESS

- Participate in party for the groom, if there is one
- Pay for own wedding attire and transportation to the wedding
- Contribute to the ushers' gift to the groom. Usually gives an individual gift to the couple expected to attend the rehearsal and the rehearsal dinner

WEDDING DAY

- Review any special seating situations with the head usher before the ceremony begins
- Greets guests as they arrive
- Seat the eldest women first if a group of guests arrive simultaneously
- Ask guests whether they are to be seated on the bride's side or the groom's side
- Offer their right arm to female guests (with the guest's escort walking behind) or ask couples to follow behind (leading couple to their seat)
- Walk to the left side of a male guest
- Hand each guest a program when they are seated
- Put the aisle runner in place after guests are seated and before the processional begins
- Know the order of seating per tradition such as special guests, grandmothers of the bride and groom, and bride's mother last
- Remove pew ribbons, one row at a time, after the ceremony
- Close windows and check pews for programs or articles left behind after the ceremony
- Are prepared to direct guests to the reception site (having extra maps available, if used)
- Look after elderly relatives or friends
- Participate in garter ceremony, if there is one, and encourage other single men to participate

POST WEDDING

- Coordinate return of rented apparel with head usher or best man

Notes:
____
____
____
____

Groomsmen and Ushers' Checklist

PRE-WEDDING PLANNING PROCESS

- Participate in party for the groom, if there is one
- Pay for own wedding attire and transportation to the wedding
- Contribute to the ushers' gift to the groom. Usually gives an individual gift to the couple expected to attend the rehearsal and the rehearsal dinner

WEDDING DAY

- Review any special seating situations with the head usher before the ceremony begins
- Greets guests as they arrive
- Seat the eldest women first if a group of guests arrive simultaneously
- Ask guests whether they are to be seated on the bride's side or the groom's side
- Offer their right arm to female guests (with the guest's escort walking behind) or ask couples to follow behind (leading couple to their seat)
- Walk to the left side of a male guest
- Hand each guest a program when they are seated
- Put the aisle runner in place after guests are seated and before the processional begins
- Know the order of seating per tradition such as special guests, grandmothers of the bride and groom, and bride's mother last
- Remove pew ribbons, one row at a time, after the ceremony
- Close windows and check pews for programs or articles left behind after the ceremony
- Are prepared to direct guests to the reception site (having extra maps available, if used)
- Look after elderly relatives or friends
- Participate in garter ceremony, if there is one, and encourage other single men to participate

POST WEDDING

- Coordinate return of rented apparel with head usher or best man

---

Notes:
____
____
____

Groomsmen and Ushers' Checklist

PRE-WEDDING PLANNING PROCESS

- Participate in party for the groom, if there is one
- Pay for own wedding attire and transportation to the wedding
- Contribute to the ushers' gift to the groom. Usually gives an individual gift to the couple expected to attend the rehearsal and the rehearsal dinner

WEDDING DAY

- Review any special seating situations with the head usher before the ceremony begins
- Greets guests as they arrive
- Seat the eldest women first if a group of guests arrive simultaneously
- Ask guests whether they are to be seated on the bride's side or the groom's side
- Offer their right arm to female guests (with the guest's escort walking behind) or ask couples to follow behind (leading couple to their seat)
- Walk to the left side of a male guest
- Hand each guest a program when they are seated
- Put the aisle runner in place after guests are seated and before the processional begins
- Know the order of seating per tradition such as special guests, grandmothers of the bride and groom, and bride's mother last
- Remove pew ribbons, one row at a time, after the ceremony
- Close windows and check pews for programs or articles left behind after the ceremony
- Are prepared to direct guests to the reception site (having extra maps available, if used)
- Look after elderly relatives or friends
- Participate in garter ceremony, if there is one, and encourage other single men to participate

POST WEDDING

- Coordinate return of rented apparel with head usher or best man

Notes:

Groomsmen and Ushers' Checklist

PRE-WEDDING PLANNING PROCESS

- Participate in party for the groom, if there is one
- Pay for own wedding attire and transportation to the wedding
- Contribute to the ushers' gift to the groom. Usually gives an individual gift to the couple expected to attend the rehearsal and the rehearsal dinner

WEDDING DAY

- Review any special seating situations with the head usher before the ceremony begins
- Greets guests as they arrive
- Seat the eldest women first if a group of guests arrive simultaneously
- Ask guests whether they are to be seated on the bride's side or the groom's side
- Offer their right arm to female guests (with the guest's escort walking behind) or ask couples to follow behind (leading couple to their seat)
- Walk to the left side of a male guest
- Hand each guest a program when they are seated
- Put the aisle runner in place after guests are seated and before the processional begins
- Know the order of seating per tradition such as special guests, grandmothers of the bride and groom, and bride's mother last
- Remove pew ribbons, one row at a time, after the ceremony
- Close windows and check pews for programs or articles left behind after the ceremony
- Are prepared to direct guests to the reception site (having extra maps available, if used)
- Look after elderly relatives or friends
- Participate in garter ceremony, if there is one, and encourage other single men to participate

POST WEDDING

- Coordinate return of rented apparel with head usher or best man

Notes:

Groomsmen and Ushers' Checklist

PRE-WEDDING PLANNING PROCESS

- Participate in party for the groom, if there is one
- Pay for own wedding attire and transportation to the wedding
- Contribute to the ushers' gift to the groom. Usually gives an individual gift to the couple expected to attend the rehearsal and the rehearsal dinner

WEDDING DAY

- Review any special seating situations with the head usher before the ceremony begins
- Greets guests as they arrive
- Seat the eldest women first if a group of guests arrive simultaneously
- Ask guests whether they are to be seated on the bride's side or the groom's side
- Offer their right arm to female guests (with the guest's escort walking behind) or ask couples to follow behind (leading couple to their seat)
- Walk to the left side of a male guest
- Hand each guest a program when they are seated
- Put the aisle runner in place after guests are seated and before the processional begins
- Know the order of seating per tradition such as special guests, grandmothers of the bride and groom, and bride's mother last
- Remove pew ribbons, one row at a time, after the ceremony
- Close windows and check pews for programs or articles left behind after the ceremony
- Are prepared to direct guests to the reception site (having extra maps available, if used)
- Look after elderly relatives or friends
- Participate in garter ceremony, if there is one, and encourage other single men to participate

POST WEDDING

- Coordinate return of rented apparel with head usher or best man

Notes:
____
____
____
____

Groomsmen and Ushers' Checklist

PRE-WEDDING PLANNING PROCESS

- Participate in party for the groom, if there is one
- Pay for own wedding attire and transportation to the wedding
- Contribute to the ushers' gift to the groom. Usually gives an individual gift to the couple expected to attend the rehearsal and the rehearsal dinner

WEDDING DAY

- Review any special seating situations with the head usher before the ceremony begins
- Greets guests as they arrive
- Seat the eldest women first if a group of guests arrive simultaneously
- Ask guests whether they are to be seated on the bride's side or the groom's side
- Offer their right arm to female guests (with the guest's escort walking behind) or ask couples to follow behind (leading couple to their seat)
- Walk to the left side of a male guest
- Hand each guest a program when they are seated
- Put the aisle runner in place after guests are seated and before the processional begins
- Know the order of seating per tradition such as special guests, grandmothers of the bride and groom, and bride's mother last
- Remove pew ribbons, one row at a time, after the ceremony
- Close windows and check pews for programs or articles left behind after the ceremony
- Are prepared to direct guests to the reception site (having extra maps available, if used)
- Look after elderly relatives or friends
- Participate in garter ceremony, if there is one, and encourage other single men to participate

POST WEDDING

- Coordinate return of rented apparel with head usher or best man

Notes:
____
____
____
____

Groomsmen and Ushers' Checklist

PRE-WEDDING PLANNING PROCESS

- Participate in party for the groom, if there is one
- Pay for own wedding attire and transportation to the wedding
- Contribute to the ushers' gift to the groom. Usually gives an individual gift to the couple expected to attend the rehearsal and the rehearsal dinner

WEDDING DAY

- Review any special seating situations with the head usher before the ceremony begins
- Greets guests as they arrive
- Seat the eldest women first if a group of guests arrive simultaneously
- Ask guests whether they are to be seated on the bride's side or the groom's side
- Offer their right arm to female guests (with the guest's escort walking behind) or ask couples to follow behind (leading couple to their seat)
- Walk to the left side of a male guest
- Hand each guest a program when they are seated
- Put the aisle runner in place after guests are seated and before the processional begins
- Know the order of seating per tradition such as special guests, grandmothers of the bride and groom, and bride's mother last
- Remove pew ribbons, one row at a time, after the ceremony
- Close windows and check pews for programs or articles left behind after the ceremony
- Are prepared to direct guests to the reception site (having extra maps available, if used)
- Look after elderly relatives or friends
- Participate in garter ceremony, if there is one, and encourage other single men to participate

POST WEDDING

- Coordinate return of rented apparel with head usher or best man

Notes:

____

____

____

Groomsmen and Ushers' Checklist

PRE-WEDDING PLANNING PROCESS

- Participate in party for the groom, if there is one
- Pay for own wedding attire and transportation to the wedding
- Contribute to the ushers' gift to the groom. Usually gives an individual gift to the couple expected to attend the rehearsal and the rehearsal dinner

WEDDING DAY

- Review any special seating situations with the head usher before the ceremony begins
- Greets guests as they arrive
- Seat the eldest women first if a group of guests arrive simultaneously
- Ask guests whether they are to be seated on the bride's side or the groom's side
- Offer their right arm to female guests (with the guest's escort walking behind) or ask couples to follow behind (leading couple to their seat)
- Walk to the left side of a male guest
- Hand each guest a program when they are seated
- Put the aisle runner in place after guests are seated and before the processional begins
- Know the order of seating per tradition such as special guests, grandmothers of the bride and groom, and bride's mother last
- Remove pew ribbons, one row at a time, after the ceremony
- Close windows and check pews for programs or articles left behind after the ceremony
- Are prepared to direct guests to the reception site (having extra maps available, if used)
- Look after elderly relatives or friends
- Participate in garter ceremony, if there is one, and encourage other single men to participate

POST WEDDING

- Coordinate return of rented apparel with head usher or best man

Notes:

Groomsmen and Ushers' Checklist

PRE-WEDDING PLANNING PROCESS

- Participate in party for the groom, if there is one
- Pay for own wedding attire and transportation to the wedding
- Contribute to the ushers' gift to the groom. Usually gives an individual gift to the couple expected to attend the rehearsal and the rehearsal dinner

WEDDING DAY

- Review any special seating situations with the head usher before the ceremony begins
- Greets guests as they arrive
- Seat the eldest women first if a group of guests arrive simultaneously
- Ask guests whether they are to be seated on the bride's side or the groom's side
- Offer their right arm to female guests (with the guest's escort walking behind) or ask couples to follow behind (leading couple to their seat)
- Walk to the left side of a male guest
- Hand each guest a program when they are seated
- Put the aisle runner in place after guests are seated and before the processional begins
- Know the order of seating per tradition such as special guests, grandmothers of the bride and groom, and bride's mother last
- Remove pew ribbons, one row at a time, after the ceremony
- Close windows and check pews for programs or articles left behind after the ceremony
- Are prepared to direct guests to the reception site (having extra maps available, if used)
- Look after elderly relatives or friends
- Participate in garter ceremony, if there is one, and encourage other single men to participate

POST WEDDING

- Coordinate return of rented apparel with head usher or best man

Notes:

____

____

____

____

Groomsmen and Ushers' Checklist

PRE-WEDDING PLANNING PROCESS

- Participate in party for the groom, if there is one
- Pay for own wedding attire and transportation to the wedding
- Contribute to the ushers' gift to the groom. Usually gives an individual gift to the couple expected to attend the rehearsal and the rehearsal dinner

WEDDING DAY

- Review any special seating situations with the head usher before the ceremony begins
- Greets guests as they arrive
- Seat the eldest women first if a group of guests arrive simultaneously
- Ask guests whether they are to be seated on the bride's side or the groom's side
- Offer their right arm to female guests (with the guest's escort walking behind) or ask couples to follow behind (leading couple to their seat)
- Walk to the left side of a male guest
- Hand each guest a program when they are seated
- Put the aisle runner in place after guests are seated and before the processional begins
- Know the order of seating per tradition such as special guests, grandmothers of the bride and groom, and bride's mother last
- Remove pew ribbons, one row at a time, after the ceremony
- Close windows and check pews for programs or articles left behind after the ceremony
- Are prepared to direct guests to the reception site (having extra maps available, if used)
- Look after elderly relatives or friends
- Participate in garter ceremony, if there is one, and encourage other single men to participate

POST WEDDING

- Coordinate return of rented apparel with head usher or best man

Notes: ____

____

____

____

Groomsmen and Ushers' Checklist

PRE-WEDDING PLANNING PROCESS

- Participate in party for the groom, if there is one
- Pay for own wedding attire and transportation to the wedding
- Contribute to the ushers' gift to the groom. Usually gives an individual gift to the couple expected to attend the rehearsal and the rehearsal dinner

WEDDING DAY

- Review any special seating situations with the head usher before the ceremony begins
- Greets guests as they arrive
- Seat the eldest women first if a group of guests arrive simultaneously
- Ask guests whether they are to be seated on the bride's side or the groom's side
- Offer their right arm to female guests (with the guest's escort walking behind) or ask couples to follow behind (leading couple to their seat)
- Walk to the left side of a male guest
- Hand each guest a program when they are seated
- Put the aisle runner in place after guests are seated and before the processional begins
- Know the order of seating per tradition such as special guests, grandmothers of the bride and groom, and bride's mother last
- Remove pew ribbons, one row at a time, after the ceremony
- Close windows and check pews for programs or articles left behind after the ceremony
- Are prepared to direct guests to the reception site (having extra maps available, if used)
- Look after elderly relatives or friends
- Participate in garter ceremony, if there is one, and encourage other single men to participate

POST WEDDING

- Coordinate return of rented apparel with head usher or best man

Notes:

Groomsmen and Ushers' Checklist

PRE-WEDDING PLANNING PROCESS

- Participate in party for the groom, if there is one
- Pay for own wedding attire and transportation to the wedding
- Contribute to the ushers' gift to the groom. Usually gives an individual gift to the couple expected to attend the rehearsal and the rehearsal dinner

WEDDING DAY

- Review any special seating situations with the head usher before the ceremony begins
- Greets guests as they arrive
- Seat the eldest women first if a group of guests arrive simultaneously
- Ask guests whether they are to be seated on the bride's side or the groom's side
- Offer their right arm to female guests (with the guest's escort walking behind) or ask couples to follow behind (leading couple to their seat)
- Walk to the left side of a male guest
- Hand each guest a program when they are seated
- Put the aisle runner in place after guests are seated and before the processional begins
- Know the order of seating per tradition such as special guests, grandmothers of the bride and groom, and bride's mother last
- Remove pew ribbons, one row at a time, after the ceremony
- Close windows and check pews for programs or articles left behind after the ceremony
- Are prepared to direct guests to the reception site (having extra maps available, if used)
- Look after elderly relatives or friends
- Participate in garter ceremony, if there is one, and encourage other single men to participate

POST WEDDING

- Coordinate return of rented apparel with head usher or best man

Notes: ____

____

____

____

Groomsmen and Ushers' Checklist

PRE-WEDDING PLANNING PROCESS

- Participate in party for the groom, if there is one
- Pay for own wedding attire and transportation to the wedding
- Contribute to the ushers' gift to the groom. Usually gives an individual gift to the couple expected to attend the rehearsal and the rehearsal dinner

WEDDING DAY

- Review any special seating situations with the head usher before the ceremony begins
- Greets guests as they arrive
- Seat the eldest women first if a group of guests arrive simultaneously
- Ask guests whether they are to be seated on the bride's side or the groom's side
- Offer their right arm to female guests (with the guest's escort walking behind) or ask couples to follow behind (leading couple to their seat)
- Walk to the left side of a male guest
- Hand each guest a program when they are seated
- Put the aisle runner in place after guests are seated and before the processional begins
- Know the order of seating per tradition such as special guests, grandmothers of the bride and groom, and bride's mother last
- Remove pew ribbons, one row at a time, after the ceremony
- Close windows and check pews for programs or articles left behind after the ceremony
- Are prepared to direct guests to the reception site (having extra maps available, if used)
- Look after elderly relatives or friends
- Participate in garter ceremony, if there is one, and encourage other single men to participate

POST WEDDING

- Coordinate return of rented apparel with head usher or best man

Notes:

Groomsmen and Ushers' Checklist

PRE-WEDDING PLANNING PROCESS

- Participate in party for the groom, if there is one
- Pay for own wedding attire and transportation to the wedding
- Contribute to the ushers' gift to the groom. Usually gives an individual gift to the couple expected to attend the rehearsal and the rehearsal dinner

WEDDING DAY

- Review any special seating situations with the head usher before the ceremony begins
- Greets guests as they arrive
- Seat the eldest women first if a group of guests arrive simultaneously
- Ask guests whether they are to be seated on the bride's side or the groom's side
- Offer their right arm to female guests (with the guest's escort walking behind) or ask couples to follow behind (leading couple to their seat)
- Walk to the left side of a male guest
- Hand each guest a program when they are seated
- Put the aisle runner in place after guests are seated and before the processional begins
- Know the order of seating per tradition such as special guests, grandmothers of the bride and groom, and bride's mother last
- Remove pew ribbons, one row at a time, after the ceremony
- Close windows and check pews for programs or articles left behind after the ceremony
- Are prepared to direct guests to the reception site (having extra maps available, if used)
- Look after elderly relatives or friends
- Participate in garter ceremony, if there is one, and encourage other single men to participate

POST WEDDING

- Coordinate return of rented apparel with head usher or best man

Notes:

Groomsmen and Ushers' Checklist

PRE-WEDDING PLANNING PROCESS

- Participate in party for the groom, if there is one
- Pay for own wedding attire and transportation to the wedding
- Contribute to the ushers' gift to the groom. Usually gives an individual gift to the couple expected to attend the rehearsal and the rehearsal dinner

WEDDING DAY

- Review any special seating situations with the head usher before the ceremony begins
- Greets guests as they arrive
- Seat the eldest women first if a group of guests arrive simultaneously
- Ask guests whether they are to be seated on the bride's side or the groom's side
- Offer their right arm to female guests (with the guest's escort walking behind) or ask couples to follow behind (leading couple to their seat)
- Walk to the left side of a male guest
- Hand each guest a program when they are seated
- Put the aisle runner in place after guests are seated and before the processional begins
- Know the order of seating per tradition such as special guests, grandmothers of the bride and groom, and bride's mother last
- Remove pew ribbons, one row at a time, after the ceremony
- Close windows and check pews for programs or articles left behind after the ceremony
- Are prepared to direct guests to the reception site (having extra maps available, if used)
- Look after elderly relatives or friends
- Participate in garter ceremony, if there is one, and encourage other single men to participate

POST WEDDING

- Coordinate return of rented apparel with head usher or best man

---

Notes:

____

____

____

Groomsmen and Ushers' Checklist

PRE-WEDDING PLANNING PROCESS

- Participate in party for the groom, if there is one
- Pay for own wedding attire and transportation to the wedding
- Contribute to the ushers' gift to the groom. Usually gives an individual gift to the couple expected to attend the rehearsal and the rehearsal dinner

WEDDING DAY

- Review any special seating situations with the head usher before the ceremony begins
- Greets guests as they arrive
- Seat the eldest women first if a group of guests arrive simultaneously
- Ask guests whether they are to be seated on the bride's side or the groom's side
- Offer their right arm to female guests (with the guest's escort walking behind) or ask couples to follow behind (leading couple to their seat)
- Walk to the left side of a male guest
- Hand each guest a program when they are seated
- Put the aisle runner in place after guests are seated and before the processional begins
- Know the order of seating per tradition such as special guests, grandmothers of the bride and groom, and bride's mother last
- Remove pew ribbons, one row at a time, after the ceremony
- Close windows and check pews for programs or articles left behind after the ceremony
- Are prepared to direct guests to the reception site (having extra maps available, if used)
- Look after elderly relatives or friends
- Participate in garter ceremony, if there is one, and encourage other single men to participate

POST WEDDING

- Coordinate return of rented apparel with head usher or best man

Notes:

Groomsmen and Ushers' Checklist

PRE-WEDDING PLANNING PROCESS

- Participate in party for the groom, if there is one
- Pay for own wedding attire and transportation to the wedding
- Contribute to the ushers' gift to the groom. Usually gives an individual gift to the couple expected to attend the rehearsal and the rehearsal dinner

WEDDING DAY

- Review any special seating situations with the head usher before the ceremony begins
- Greets guests as they arrive
- Seat the eldest women first if a group of guests arrive simultaneously
- Ask guests whether they are to be seated on the bride's side or the groom's side
- Offer their right arm to female guests (with the guest's escort walking behind) or ask couples to follow behind (leading couple to their seat)
- Walk to the left side of a male guest
- Hand each guest a program when they are seated
- Put the aisle runner in place after guests are seated and before the processional begins
- Know the order of seating per tradition such as special guests, grandmothers of the bride and groom, and bride's mother last
- Remove pew ribbons, one row at a time, after the ceremony
- Close windows and check pews for programs or articles left behind after the ceremony
- Are prepared to direct guests to the reception site (having extra maps available, if used)
- Look after elderly relatives or friends
- Participate in garter ceremony, if there is one, and encourage other single men to participate

POST WEDDING

- Coordinate return of rented apparel with head usher or best man

Notes:
____
____
____
____

Groomsmen and Ushers' Checklist

PRE-WEDDING PLANNING PROCESS

- Participate in party for the groom, if there is one
- Pay for own wedding attire and transportation to the wedding
- Contribute to the ushers' gift to the groom. Usually gives an individual gift to the couple expected to attend the rehearsal and the rehearsal dinner

WEDDING DAY

- Review any special seating situations with the head usher before the ceremony begins
- Greets guests as they arrive
- Seat the eldest women first if a group of guests arrive simultaneously
- Ask guests whether they are to be seated on the bride's side or the groom's side
- Offer their right arm to female guests (with the guest's escort walking behind) or ask couples to follow behind (leading couple to their seat)
- Walk to the left side of a male guest
- Hand each guest a program when they are seated
- Put the aisle runner in place after guests are seated and before the processional begins
- Know the order of seating per tradition such as special guests, grandmothers of the bride and groom, and bride's mother last
- Remove pew ribbons, one row at a time, after the ceremony
- Close windows and check pews for programs or articles left behind after the ceremony
- Are prepared to direct guests to the reception site (having extra maps available, if used)
- Look after elderly relatives or friends
- Participate in garter ceremony, if there is one, and encourage other single men to participate

POST WEDDING

- Coordinate return of rented apparel with head usher or best man

Notes:
____
____
____
____

Groomsmen and Ushers' Checklist

PRE-WEDDING PLANNING PROCESS

- Participate in party for the groom, if there is one
- Pay for own wedding attire and transportation to the wedding
- Contribute to the ushers' gift to the groom. Usually gives an individual gift to the couple expected to attend the rehearsal and the rehearsal dinner

WEDDING DAY

- Review any special seating situations with the head usher before the ceremony begins
- Greets guests as they arrive
- Seat the eldest women first if a group of guests arrive simultaneously
- Ask guests whether they are to be seated on the bride's side or the groom's side
- Offer their right arm to female guests (with the guest's escort walking behind) or ask couples to follow behind (leading couple to their seat)
- Walk to the left side of a male guest
- Hand each guest a program when they are seated
- Put the aisle runner in place after guests are seated and before the processional begins
- Know the order of seating per tradition such as special guests, grandmothers of the bride and groom, and bride's mother last
- Remove pew ribbons, one row at a time, after the ceremony
- Close windows and check pews for programs or articles left behind after the ceremony
- Are prepared to direct guests to the reception site (having extra maps available, if used)
- Look after elderly relatives or friends
- Participate in garter ceremony, if there is one, and encourage other single men to participate

POST WEDDING

- Coordinate return of rented apparel with head usher or best man

Notes:

Groomsmen and Ushers' Checklist

PRE-WEDDING PLANNING PROCESS

- Participate in party for the groom, if there is one
- Pay for own wedding attire and transportation to the wedding
- Contribute to the ushers' gift to the groom. Usually gives an individual gift to the couple expected to attend the rehearsal and the rehearsal dinner

WEDDING DAY

- Review any special seating situations with the head usher before the ceremony begins
- Greets guests as they arrive
- Seat the eldest women first if a group of guests arrive simultaneously
- Ask guests whether they are to be seated on the bride's side or the groom's side
- Offer their right arm to female guests (with the guest's escort walking behind) or ask couples to follow behind (leading couple to their seat)
- Walk to the left side of a male guest
- Hand each guest a program when they are seated
- Put the aisle runner in place after guests are seated and before the processional begins
- Know the order of seating per tradition such as special guests, grandmothers of the bride and groom, and bride's mother last
- Remove pew ribbons, one row at a time, after the ceremony
- Close windows and check pews for programs or articles left behind after the ceremony
- Are prepared to direct guests to the reception site (having extra maps available, if used)
- Look after elderly relatives or friends
- Participate in garter ceremony, if there is one, and encourage other single men to participate

POST WEDDING

- Coordinate return of rented apparel with head usher or best man

Notes:
____
____
____
____

Groomsmen and Ushers' Checklist

PRE-WEDDING PLANNING PROCESS

- Participate in party for the groom, if there is one
- Pay for own wedding attire and transportation to the wedding
- Contribute to the ushers' gift to the groom. Usually gives an individual gift to the couple expected to attend the rehearsal and the rehearsal dinner

WEDDING DAY

- Review any special seating situations with the head usher before the ceremony begins
- Greets guests as they arrive
- Seat the eldest women first if a group of guests arrive simultaneously
- Ask guests whether they are to be seated on the bride's side or the groom's side
- Offer their right arm to female guests (with the guest's escort walking behind) or ask couples to follow behind (leading couple to their seat)
- Walk to the left side of a male guest
- Hand each guest a program when they are seated
- Put the aisle runner in place after guests are seated and before the processional begins
- Know the order of seating per tradition such as special guests, grandmothers of the bride and groom, and bride's mother last
- Remove pew ribbons, one row at a time, after the ceremony
- Close windows and check pews for programs or articles left behind after the ceremony
- Are prepared to direct guests to the reception site (having extra maps available, if used)
- Look after elderly relatives or friends
- Participate in garter ceremony, if there is one, and encourage other single men to participate

POST WEDDING

- Coordinate return of rented apparel with head usher or best man

Notes:
____
____
____
____

Groomsmen and Ushers' Checklist

PRE-WEDDING PLANNING PROCESS

- Participate in party for the groom, if there is one
- Pay for own wedding attire and transportation to the wedding
- Contribute to the ushers' gift to the groom. Usually gives an individual gift to the couple expected to attend the rehearsal and the rehearsal dinner

WEDDING DAY

- Review any special seating situations with the head usher before the ceremony begins
- Greets guests as they arrive
- Seat the eldest women first if a group of guests arrive simultaneously
- Ask guests whether they are to be seated on the bride's side or the groom's side
- Offer their right arm to female guests (with the guest's escort walking behind) or ask couples to follow behind (leading couple to their seat)
- Walk to the left side of a male guest
- Hand each guest a program when they are seated
- Put the aisle runner in place after guests are seated and before the processional begins
- Know the order of seating per tradition such as special guests, grandmothers of the bride and groom, and bride's mother last
- Remove pew ribbons, one row at a time, after the ceremony
- Close windows and check pews for programs or articles left behind after the ceremony
- Are prepared to direct guests to the reception site (having extra maps available, if used)
- Look after elderly relatives or friends
- Participate in garter ceremony, if there is one, and encourage other single men to participate

POST WEDDING

- Coordinate return of rented apparel with head usher or best man

Notes:
____
____
____
____

Groomsmen and Ushers' Checklist

PRE-WEDDING PLANNING PROCESS

- Participate in party for the groom, if there is one
- Pay for own wedding attire and transportation to the wedding
- Contribute to the ushers' gift to the groom. Usually gives an individual gift to the couple expected to attend the rehearsal and the rehearsal dinner

WEDDING DAY

- Review any special seating situations with the head usher before the ceremony begins
- Greets guests as they arrive
- Seat the eldest women first if a group of guests arrive simultaneously
- Ask guests whether they are to be seated on the bride's side or the groom's side
- Offer their right arm to female guests (with the guest's escort walking behind) or ask couples to follow behind (leading couple to their seat)
- Walk to the left side of a male guest
- Hand each guest a program when they are seated
- Put the aisle runner in place after guests are seated and before the processional begins
- Know the order of seating per tradition such as special guests, grandmothers of the bride and groom, and bride's mother last
- Remove pew ribbons, one row at a time, after the ceremony
- Close windows and check pews for programs or articles left behind after the ceremony
- Are prepared to direct guests to the reception site (having extra maps available, if used)
- Look after elderly relatives or friends
- Participate in garter ceremony, if there is one, and encourage other single men to participate

POST WEDDING

- Coordinate return of rented apparel with head usher or best man

Notes:

Groomsmen and Ushers' Checklist

PRE-WEDDING PLANNING PROCESS

- Participate in party for the groom, if there is one
- Pay for own wedding attire and transportation to the wedding
- Contribute to the ushers' gift to the groom. Usually gives an individual gift to the couple expected to attend the rehearsal and the rehearsal dinner

WEDDING DAY

- Review any special seating situations with the head usher before the ceremony begins
- Greets guests as they arrive
- Seat the eldest women first if a group of guests arrive simultaneously
- Ask guests whether they are to be seated on the bride's side or the groom's side
- Offer their right arm to female guests (with the guest's escort walking behind) or ask couples to follow behind (leading couple to their seat)
- Walk to the left side of a male guest
- Hand each guest a program when they are seated
- Put the aisle runner in place after guests are seated and before the processional begins
- Know the order of seating per tradition such as special guests, grandmothers of the bride and groom, and bride's mother last
- Remove pew ribbons, one row at a time, after the ceremony
- Close windows and check pews for programs or articles left behind after the ceremony
- Are prepared to direct guests to the reception site (having extra maps available, if used)
- Look after elderly relatives or friends
- Participate in garter ceremony, if there is one, and encourage other single men to participate

POST WEDDING

- Coordinate return of rented apparel with head usher or best man

Notes:

Groomsmen and Ushers' Checklist

PRE-WEDDING PLANNING PROCESS

- Participate in party for the groom, if there is one
- Pay for own wedding attire and transportation to the wedding
- Contribute to the ushers' gift to the groom. Usually gives an individual gift to the couple expected to attend the rehearsal and the rehearsal dinner

WEDDING DAY

- Review any special seating situations with the head usher before the ceremony begins
- Greets guests as they arrive
- Seat the eldest women first if a group of guests arrive simultaneously
- Ask guests whether they are to be seated on the bride's side or the groom's side
- Offer their right arm to female guests (with the guest's escort walking behind) or ask couples to follow behind (leading couple to their seat)
- Walk to the left side of a male guest
- Hand each guest a program when they are seated
- Put the aisle runner in place after guests are seated and before the processional begins
- Know the order of seating per tradition such as special guests, grandmothers of the bride and groom, and bride's mother last
- Remove pew ribbons, one row at a time, after the ceremony
- Close windows and check pews for programs or articles left behind after the ceremony
- Are prepared to direct guests to the reception site (having extra maps available, if used)
- Look after elderly relatives or friends
- Participate in garter ceremony, if there is one, and encourage other single men to participate

POST WEDDING

- Coordinate return of rented apparel with head usher or best man

Notes:
____
____
____
____

Groomsmen and Ushers' Checklist

PRE-WEDDING PLANNING PROCESS

- Participate in party for the groom, if there is one
- Pay for own wedding attire and transportation to the wedding
- Contribute to the ushers' gift to the groom. Usually gives an individual gift to the couple expected to attend the rehearsal and the rehearsal dinner

WEDDING DAY

- Review any special seating situations with the head usher before the ceremony begins
- Greets guests as they arrive
- Seat the eldest women first if a group of guests arrive simultaneously
- Ask guests whether they are to be seated on the bride's side or the groom's side
- Offer their right arm to female guests (with the guest's escort walking behind) or ask couples to follow behind (leading couple to their seat)
- Walk to the left side of a male guest
- Hand each guest a program when they are seated
- Put the aisle runner in place after guests are seated and before the processional begins
- Know the order of seating per tradition such as special guests, grandmothers of the bride and groom, and bride's mother last
- Remove pew ribbons, one row at a time, after the ceremony
- Close windows and check pews for programs or articles left behind after the ceremony
- Are prepared to direct guests to the reception site (having extra maps available, if used)
- Look after elderly relatives or friends
- Participate in garter ceremony, if there is one, and encourage other single men to participate

POST WEDDING

- Coordinate return of rented apparel with head usher or best man

Notes:

Groomsmen and Ushers' Checklist

PRE-WEDDING PLANNING PROCESS

- Participate in party for the groom, if there is one
- Pay for own wedding attire and transportation to the wedding
- Contribute to the ushers' gift to the groom. Usually gives an individual gift to the couple expected to attend the rehearsal and the rehearsal dinner

WEDDING DAY

- Review any special seating situations with the head usher before the ceremony begins
- Greets guests as they arrive
- Seat the eldest women first if a group of guests arrive simultaneously
- Ask guests whether they are to be seated on the bride's side or the groom's side
- Offer their right arm to female guests (with the guest's escort walking behind) or ask couples to follow behind (leading couple to their seat)
- Walk to the left side of a male guest
- Hand each guest a program when they are seated
- Put the aisle runner in place after guests are seated and before the processional begins
- Know the order of seating per tradition such as special guests, grandmothers of the bride and groom, and bride's mother last
- Remove pew ribbons, one row at a time, after the ceremony
- Close windows and check pews for programs or articles left behind after the ceremony
- Are prepared to direct guests to the reception site (having extra maps available, if used)
- Look after elderly relatives or friends
- Participate in garter ceremony, if there is one, and encourage other single men to participate

POST WEDDING

- Coordinate return of rented apparel with head usher or best man

Notes:
____
____
____
____

Groomsmen and Ushers' Checklist

PRE-WEDDING PLANNING PROCESS

- Participate in party for the groom, if there is one
- Pay for own wedding attire and transportation to the wedding
- Contribute to the ushers' gift to the groom. Usually gives an individual gift to the couple expected to attend the rehearsal and the rehearsal dinner

WEDDING DAY

- Review any special seating situations with the head usher before the ceremony begins
- Greets guests as they arrive
- Seat the eldest women first if a group of guests arrive simultaneously
- Ask guests whether they are to be seated on the bride's side or the groom's side
- Offer their right arm to female guests (with the guest's escort walking behind) or ask couples to follow behind (leading couple to their seat)
- Walk to the left side of a male guest
- Hand each guest a program when they are seated
- Put the aisle runner in place after guests are seated and before the processional begins
- Know the order of seating per tradition such as special guests, grandmothers of the bride and groom, and bride's mother last
- Remove pew ribbons, one row at a time, after the ceremony
- Close windows and check pews for programs or articles left behind after the ceremony
- Are prepared to direct guests to the reception site (having extra maps available, if used)
- Look after elderly relatives or friends
- Participate in garter ceremony, if there is one, and encourage other single men to participate

POST WEDDING

- Coordinate return of rented apparel with head usher or best man

Notes: ____

____

____

____

Groomsmen and Ushers' Checklist

PRE-WEDDING PLANNING PROCESS

- Participate in party for the groom, if there is one
- Pay for own wedding attire and transportation to the wedding
- Contribute to the ushers' gift to the groom. Usually gives an individual gift to the couple expected to attend the rehearsal and the rehearsal dinner

WEDDING DAY

- Review any special seating situations with the head usher before the ceremony begins
- Greets guests as they arrive
- Seat the eldest women first if a group of guests arrive simultaneously
- Ask guests whether they are to be seated on the bride's side or the groom's side
- Offer their right arm to female guests (with the guest's escort walking behind) or ask couples to follow behind (leading couple to their seat)
- Walk to the left side of a male guest
- Hand each guest a program when they are seated
- Put the aisle runner in place after guests are seated and before the processional begins
- Know the order of seating per tradition such as special guests, grandmothers of the bride and groom, and bride's mother last
- Remove pew ribbons, one row at a time, after the ceremony
- Close windows and check pews for programs or articles left behind after the ceremony
- Are prepared to direct guests to the reception site (having extra maps available, if used)
- Look after elderly relatives or friends
- Participate in garter ceremony, if there is one, and encourage other single men to participate

POST WEDDING

- Coordinate return of rented apparel with head usher or best man

Notes:
____
____
____
____

Groomsmen and Ushers' Checklist

PRE-WEDDING PLANNING PROCESS

- Participate in party for the groom, if there is one
- Pay for own wedding attire and transportation to the wedding
- Contribute to the ushers' gift to the groom. Usually gives an individual gift to the couple expected to attend the rehearsal and the rehearsal dinner

WEDDING DAY

- Review any special seating situations with the head usher before the ceremony begins
- Greets guests as they arrive
- Seat the eldest women first if a group of guests arrive simultaneously
- Ask guests whether they are to be seated on the bride's side or the groom's side
- Offer their right arm to female guests (with the guest's escort walking behind) or ask couples to follow behind (leading couple to their seat)
- Walk to the left side of a male guest
- Hand each guest a program when they are seated
- Put the aisle runner in place after guests are seated and before the processional begins
- Know the order of seating per tradition such as special guests, grandmothers of the bride and groom, and bride's mother last
- Remove pew ribbons, one row at a time, after the ceremony
- Close windows and check pews for programs or articles left behind after the ceremony
- Are prepared to direct guests to the reception site (having extra maps available, if used)
- Look after elderly relatives or friends
- Participate in garter ceremony, if there is one, and encourage other single men to participate

POST WEDDING

- Coordinate return of rented apparel with head usher or best man

Notes:

Groomsmen and Ushers' Checklist

PRE-WEDDING PLANNING PROCESS

- Participate in party for the groom, if there is one
- Pay for own wedding attire and transportation to the wedding
- Contribute to the ushers' gift to the groom. Usually gives an individual gift to the couple expected to attend the rehearsal and the rehearsal dinner

WEDDING DAY

- Review any special seating situations with the head usher before the ceremony begins
- Greets guests as they arrive
- Seat the eldest women first if a group of guests arrive simultaneously
- Ask guests whether they are to be seated on the bride's side or the groom's side
- Offer their right arm to female guests (with the guest's escort walking behind) or ask couples to follow behind (leading couple to their seat)
- Walk to the left side of a male guest
- Hand each guest a program when they are seated
- Put the aisle runner in place after guests are seated and before the processional begins
- Know the order of seating per tradition such as special guests, grandmothers of the bride and groom, and bride's mother last
- Remove pew ribbons, one row at a time, after the ceremony
- Close windows and check pews for programs or articles left behind after the ceremony
- Are prepared to direct guests to the reception site (having extra maps available, if used)
- Look after elderly relatives or friends
- Participate in garter ceremony, if there is one, and encourage other single men to participate

POST WEDDING

- Coordinate return of rented apparel with head usher or best man

Notes:
____
____
____
____

Groomsmen and Ushers' Checklist

PRE-WEDDING PLANNING PROCESS

- Participate in party for the groom, if there is one
- Pay for own wedding attire and transportation to the wedding
- Contribute to the ushers' gift to the groom. Usually gives an individual gift to the couple expected to attend the rehearsal and the rehearsal dinner

WEDDING DAY

- Review any special seating situations with the head usher before the ceremony begins
- Greets guests as they arrive
- Seat the eldest women first if a group of guests arrive simultaneously
- Ask guests whether they are to be seated on the bride's side or the groom's side
- Offer their right arm to female guests (with the guest's escort walking behind) or ask couples to follow behind (leading couple to their seat)
- Walk to the left side of a male guest
- Hand each guest a program when they are seated
- Put the aisle runner in place after guests are seated and before the processional begins
- Know the order of seating per tradition such as special guests, grandmothers of the bride and groom, and bride's mother last
- Remove pew ribbons, one row at a time, after the ceremony
- Close windows and check pews for programs or articles left behind after the ceremony
- Are prepared to direct guests to the reception site (having extra maps available, if used)
- Look after elderly relatives or friends
- Participate in garter ceremony, if there is one, and encourage other single men to participate

POST WEDDING

- Coordinate return of rented apparel with head usher or best man

Notes:

Groomsmen and Ushers' Checklist

PRE-WEDDING PLANNING PROCESS

- Participate in party for the groom, if there is one
- Pay for own wedding attire and transportation to the wedding
- Contribute to the ushers' gift to the groom. Usually gives an individual gift to the couple expected to attend the rehearsal and the rehearsal dinner

WEDDING DAY

- Review any special seating situations with the head usher before the ceremony begins
- Greets guests as they arrive
- Seat the eldest women first if a group of guests arrive simultaneously
- Ask guests whether they are to be seated on the bride's side or the groom's side
- Offer their right arm to female guests (with the guest's escort walking behind) or ask couples to follow behind (leading couple to their seat)
- Walk to the left side of a male guest
- Hand each guest a program when they are seated
- Put the aisle runner in place after guests are seated and before the processional begins
- Know the order of seating per tradition such as special guests, grandmothers of the bride and groom, and bride's mother last
- Remove pew ribbons, one row at a time, after the ceremony
- Close windows and check pews for programs or articles left behind after the ceremony
- Are prepared to direct guests to the reception site (having extra maps available, if used)
- Look after elderly relatives or friends
- Participate in garter ceremony, if there is one, and encourage other single men to participate

POST WEDDING

- Coordinate return of rented apparel with head usher or best man

Notes:

Groomsmen and Ushers' Checklist

PRE-WEDDING PLANNING PROCESS

- Participate in party for the groom, if there is one
- Pay for own wedding attire and transportation to the wedding
- Contribute to the ushers' gift to the groom. Usually gives an individual gift to the couple expected to attend the rehearsal and the rehearsal dinner

WEDDING DAY

- Review any special seating situations with the head usher before the ceremony begins
- Greets guests as they arrive
- Seat the eldest women first if a group of guests arrive simultaneously
- Ask guests whether they are to be seated on the bride's side or the groom's side
- Offer their right arm to female guests (with the guest's escort walking behind) or ask couples to follow behind (leading couple to their seat)
- Walk to the left side of a male guest
- Hand each guest a program when they are seated
- Put the aisle runner in place after guests are seated and before the processional begins
- Know the order of seating per tradition such as special guests, grandmothers of the bride and groom, and bride's mother last
- Remove pew ribbons, one row at a time, after the ceremony
- Close windows and check pews for programs or articles left behind after the ceremony
- Are prepared to direct guests to the reception site (having extra maps available, if used)
- Look after elderly relatives or friends
- Participate in garter ceremony, if there is one, and encourage other single men to participate

POST WEDDING

- Coordinate return of rented apparel with head usher or best man

Notes:

Groomsmen and Ushers' Checklist

PRE-WEDDING PLANNING PROCESS

- Participate in party for the groom, if there is one
- Pay for own wedding attire and transportation to the wedding
- Contribute to the ushers' gift to the groom. Usually gives an individual gift to the couple expected to attend the rehearsal and the rehearsal dinner

WEDDING DAY

- Review any special seating situations with the head usher before the ceremony begins
- Greets guests as they arrive
- Seat the eldest women first if a group of guests arrive simultaneously
- Ask guests whether they are to be seated on the bride's side or the groom's side
- Offer their right arm to female guests (with the guest's escort walking behind) or ask couples to follow behind (leading couple to their seat)
- Walk to the left side of a male guest
- Hand each guest a program when they are seated
- Put the aisle runner in place after guests are seated and before the processional begins
- Know the order of seating per tradition such as special guests, grandmothers of the bride and groom, and bride's mother last
- Remove pew ribbons, one row at a time, after the ceremony
- Close windows and check pews for programs or articles left behind after the ceremony
- Are prepared to direct guests to the reception site (having extra maps available, if used)
- Look after elderly relatives or friends
- Participate in garter ceremony, if there is one, and encourage other single men to participate

POST WEDDING

- Coordinate return of rented apparel with head usher or best man

Notes:
____
____
____
____

Groomsmen and Ushers' Checklist

PRE-WEDDING PLANNING PROCESS

- Participate in party for the groom, if there is one
- Pay for own wedding attire and transportation to the wedding
- Contribute to the ushers' gift to the groom. Usually gives an individual gift to the couple expected to attend the rehearsal and the rehearsal dinner

WEDDING DAY

- Review any special seating situations with the head usher before the ceremony begins
- Greets guests as they arrive
- Seat the eldest women first if a group of guests arrive simultaneously
- Ask guests whether they are to be seated on the bride's side or the groom's side
- Offer their right arm to female guests (with the guest's escort walking behind) or ask couples to follow behind (leading couple to their seat)
- Walk to the left side of a male guest
- Hand each guest a program when they are seated
- Put the aisle runner in place after guests are seated and before the processional begins
- Know the order of seating per tradition such as special guests, grandmothers of the bride and groom, and bride's mother last
- Remove pew ribbons, one row at a time, after the ceremony
- Close windows and check pews for programs or articles left behind after the ceremony
- Are prepared to direct guests to the reception site (having extra maps available, if used)
- Look after elderly relatives or friends
- Participate in garter ceremony, if there is one, and encourage other single men to participate

POST WEDDING

- Coordinate return of rented apparel with head usher or best man

Notes:

Groomsmen and Ushers' Checklist

PRE-WEDDING PLANNING PROCESS

- Participate in party for the groom, if there is one
- Pay for own wedding attire and transportation to the wedding
- Contribute to the ushers' gift to the groom. Usually gives an individual gift to the couple expected to attend the rehearsal and the rehearsal dinner

WEDDING DAY

- Review any special seating situations with the head usher before the ceremony begins
- Greets guests as they arrive
- Seat the eldest women first if a group of guests arrive simultaneously
- Ask guests whether they are to be seated on the bride's side or the groom's side
- Offer their right arm to female guests (with the guest's escort walking behind) or ask couples to follow behind (leading couple to their seat)
- Walk to the left side of a male guest
- Hand each guest a program when they are seated
- Put the aisle runner in place after guests are seated and before the processional begins
- Know the order of seating per tradition such as special guests, grandmothers of the bride and groom, and bride's mother last
- Remove pew ribbons, one row at a time, after the ceremony
- Close windows and check pews for programs or articles left behind after the ceremony
- Are prepared to direct guests to the reception site (having extra maps available, if used)
- Look after elderly relatives or friends
- Participate in garter ceremony, if there is one, and encourage other single men to participate

POST WEDDING

- Coordinate return of rented apparel with head usher or best man

Notes:

Groomsmen and Ushers' Checklist

PRE-WEDDING PLANNING PROCESS

- Participate in party for the groom, if there is one
- Pay for own wedding attire and transportation to the wedding
- Contribute to the ushers' gift to the groom. Usually gives an individual gift to the couple expected to attend the rehearsal and the rehearsal dinner

WEDDING DAY

- Review any special seating situations with the head usher before the ceremony begins
- Greets guests as they arrive
- Seat the eldest women first if a group of guests arrive simultaneously
- Ask guests whether they are to be seated on the bride's side or the groom's side
- Offer their right arm to female guests (with the guest's escort walking behind) or ask couples to follow behind (leading couple to their seat)
- Walk to the left side of a male guest
- Hand each guest a program when they are seated
- Put the aisle runner in place after guests are seated and before the processional begins
- Know the order of seating per tradition such as special guests, grandmothers of the bride and groom, and bride's mother last
- Remove pew ribbons, one row at a time, after the ceremony
- Close windows and check pews for programs or articles left behind after the ceremony
- Are prepared to direct guests to the reception site (having extra maps available, if used)
- Look after elderly relatives or friends
- Participate in garter ceremony, if there is one, and encourage other single men to participate

POST WEDDING

- Coordinate return of rented apparel with head usher or best man

Notes: ____

____

____

____

Groomsmen and Ushers' Checklist

PRE-WEDDING PLANNING PROCESS

- Participate in party for the groom, if there is one
- Pay for own wedding attire and transportation to the wedding
- Contribute to the ushers' gift to the groom. Usually gives an individual gift to the couple expected to attend the rehearsal and the rehearsal dinner

WEDDING DAY

- Review any special seating situations with the head usher before the ceremony begins
- Greets guests as they arrive
- Seat the eldest women first if a group of guests arrive simultaneously
- Ask guests whether they are to be seated on the bride's side or the groom's side
- Offer their right arm to female guests (with the guest's escort walking behind) or ask couples to follow behind (leading couple to their seat)
- Walk to the left side of a male guest
- Hand each guest a program when they are seated
- Put the aisle runner in place after guests are seated and before the processional begins
- Know the order of seating per tradition such as special guests, grandmothers of the bride and groom, and bride's mother last
- Remove pew ribbons, one row at a time, after the ceremony
- Close windows and check pews for programs or articles left behind after the ceremony
- Are prepared to direct guests to the reception site (having extra maps available, if used)
- Look after elderly relatives or friends
- Participate in garter ceremony, if there is one, and encourage other single men to participate

POST WEDDING

- Coordinate return of rented apparel with head usher or best man

Notes:
____
____
____
____